It's How You Play the Game

It's How You Play the Game

Duffy Robbins

VICTOR BOOKS®
A DIVISION OF SCRIPTURE PRESS PUBLICATIONS INC.
USA CANADA ENGLAND

Scripture quotations, unless otherwise indicated, are from the Holy Bible, New International Version, © 1973, 1978, 1984, International Bible Society. Used by permission of Zondervan Bible Publishers.

Library of Congress Cataloging-in-Publication Data

Robbins, Duffy.
It's how you play the game / by David Robbins.
p. cm. – Straight talk series ; 2)
Summary: The author describes one of his favorite Biblical heroes, David, King of Israel, and discusses how teenagers can apply the lessons of David's life to their own lives.
ISBN 0-89693-856-5
1. David, King of Israel—Sermons. 2. Youth sermons.
[1. Conduct of life. 2. Christian life. 3. David, King of Israel.]
I. Title. II. Series.
BS580.D3R58 1991 91-13924
252'.55—dc20 CIP
AC

1 2 3 4 5 6 7 8 9 10 Printing/Year 95 94 93 92 91

Contents

DEDICATION

Every year it is my great privilege to share the good news of God's love with teenagers all over North America and in various parts of the globe. All in all, it has added up to some incredible moments in places like Toronto, Ontario; St. Simons Island, Georgia; Orange County, California; Estes Park, Colorado; Sydney, Australia; Lake Junaluska, North Carolina; Motley, Minnesota; Brevard, North Carolina; Orlando, Florida; Berlin, Germany; Edmonton, Alberta; Indianapolis, Indiana; and Panama City, Florida.

To all of those students over the years and across the miles who have listened, laughed, thought, and responded, thanks for your warmth and your openness. It isn't possible to exercise the gift of speaking unless folks are willing to exercise the gift of listening. Your willingness to listen to me has been a gift indeed.

1. My Hero

The Lord has sought out a man after His own heart and appointed him leader of His people" (1 Samuel 13:14).

If I were to ask you what name is mentioned in the Bible more than any other, I know exactly how you'd answer:

"I really don't give a rip."

But just for fun, take a guess. Whose name is mentioned in the Bible more than anyone else's?

God, right? Well, yes; but what about just normal human beings? Which human being is mentioned by name in the Bible more than any other?

Jesus? No, but nice try. (He's almost always a safe answer for Sunday-School-type questions.)

OK, how about Moses? No, but that's another good name from the Flannelgraph Hall of Fame.

What about Abraham? No.

Pharaoh? No.

David? Definitely not.

Elvis? Very funny.

Jacob? No.

Peter? No.

Paul? No.

Peter, Paul, and Mary? No.

Joshua? Yes! Fantastic! You're good! Nice work! Except that it wasn't Joshua either. That was just a little trick to pay you back for the Elvis comment.

One last time: What name is mentioned in the Bible more than any other?

Give up? Well, the answer is David.

What? OK, I know I listed David's name earlier and said no. But that was just to add to the suspense. David is really and truly our man. It's his name that is mentioned in the Bible more than any other.

In fact, for those of you who are big-time into trivia, you might be interested to know that Abraham's story spans some 18 chapters of the Old Testament, much more than Moses'. Jacob's story takes 25 chapters. (I dare you to try to slide this information into a conversation this week at school.) But David's story is told over the course of 61 chapters of the Old Testament. Sixty-one! Actually, if you want to get technical, you have to add another 72 or 73 Psalms written by David. This guy David is everywhere.

Rosanne, Madonna, and A Prophet Named Elisha

I have to confess that David has always been my hero. And why not? To begin with, all of us have heroes of one kind or another. Your hero might be Rosanne Barr, Tom Cruise, Arsenio Hall, or Pee-wee Herman. Maybe your hero is Michael Jordan because you're really into basketball. All of us have heroes.

I guess that's why, over the last several years, I've begun to identify certain characters from the Bible who have really become my heroes—people I can look up to. For example, there's Elisha, a great prophet of God who walked the pages of 2 Kings in the Old Testament. He wasn't just a prophet. He was a bald-headed prophet. (If you look at my picture on the back cover of this book, you will note that we have a similar hairstyle!)

One of my favorite Elisha stories is in 2 Kings 2:23-24:

> From there Elisha went up to Bethel. As he was walking along the road, some youths came out of the town and jeered at him. "Go on up, you baldhead!" He turned around, looked at them, and called down a curse on them in the name of the Lord. Then two [she] bears [that's right, two female bears] came out of the woods and mauled forty-two of the youths.

Ah, yes. I just love that story. What a blessing! In fact, I once used this as a children's sermon in our church. The flannelgraph was gruesome, but I'll tell you what: Those kids started showing me some respect!

A Duffer Named David

Granted, David probably had a full head of hair. And, to my knowledge, his only encounter with a bear (sex unknown) ended up with the bear on the short end. (See 1 Samuel 17:34-35.) But he still ranks right up there on my hero list. David stands out as one of the most powerful personalities in all of Scripture, identified by some as one of the Bible's greatest sinners and one of the Bible's greatest saints. We're talking about a guy described in Scripture as a man after God's own heart. That's pretty hot stuff to write in anybody's yearbook.

But, to be honest, what really draws me to this man David is much more basic: We have the same name. My real, honest-to-goodness name is David. David William Robbins.

People are always asking me, "How *did* you get a name like Duffy anyway?" They pose the question the way you would ask someone with a cast what happened to his leg. I have to explain that the nickname Duffy was given me by my parents during my first few months of life. My dad played a lot of golf, and a beginner in golf is called a duffer. So every now and then, my Dad would say to Mom, "Hey, we better put the Duffer down for a nap." And, of course, the Duffer eventually became Duffy.

It hasn't been easy either. When I was a little kid, my friends in kindergarten never really got the hang of saying my name right. So I had to go through life answering to names like Guppy, Daffy, and Ducky. (Hey, it's not funny.) Try growing up with a name that sounds like a cartoon character or a small fish. Even now I sometimes have to accept a long-distance call from an operator who asks for Buffy Robbins. Good grief!

Most of all, though, when I look at this man David, I begin to realize that I share not only his name but also his struggles. I share his failures. I share his temptations. And, every now and then, I even share his victories.

That's what makes the following chapters so important. David's life is a mirror of our own. When we look at him, we don't see some bear-killing, giant-slaying, bald-headed prophet who lived 3,000 years ago. We see ourselves. And we see the God who takes us as we are, with all of our weaknesses and shortcomings, and dares to call us His own.

Don't read this book if you like your biblical heroes neat and clean. There are some ugly episodes in David's story. This is not *Mr. Rogers Meets God.* David's story has chapters of adultery, failure, murder, and even mass murder. But it also includes chapters of forgiveness, triumph, and celebration. Basically, what we will discover is how God worked in one man's life to make him into the person He created him to be.

It's How You Play the Game

When I was in fifth grade, the coach of our neighborhood football team used to tell us, "Guys, it's not whether you win or lose; it's how you play the game." Translated, I think what he was saying was, "Guys, never mind that this team has scored on us with everybody but their cheerleaders. You're doing your best, you're learning character, and I'm committed to you."

Frankly, when we were sitting there at halftime with bloody noses, bandaged knees and banged up egos, that didn't help very much. But now, as I look back, I can understand what that coach meant. He was saying that there will come a time when nobody will really care whether we won this game or not, or even who made a good play or a bad play. What will matter is how we played the game—whether we learned from our mistakes, whether we continued to push for the goal, whether we got up to try again after we'd been knocked down.

Basically, that is the lesson of David's life. He won some, and he lost some; but the key was how he played the game.

I found out several years ago that the dictionary definition of a duffer is not very flattering. It means one who is stupid and dull, not exactly the stuff you list on your resumé. But my father actually named me David. It's a Hebrew word that means *beloved.*

David's story is the saga of a loving heavenly Father who walks with His children on the journey from being duffers to becoming Davids. It's the story of a God who coaches His children through victories and defeats and encourages them each time they fall to get up and move on toward the goal. The neat fact is that the very same God who loved that David 3,000 years ago loves this David today even as I write these words. And He loves you too!

My prayer as you read this book is that you'll laugh some, learn a little, and think a lot; that you'll get to meet people like Mephibosheth and Saul; and that maybe (for extra credit) you'll discover how to identify a she-bear in full charge. But most of all, I pray that God will use these chapters to encourage you in your walk with Jesus Christ—even when you fall. My prayer is that for all those times when you're feeling down and falling behind, you will remember that you have a loving and patient Father in heaven who is saying, "It's not whether you win or lose; it's how you play the game."

SECTION ONE:
SAUL—THE WASTED PAPER CLIP

Saul was afraid of David, because the Lord was with David but had left Saul. In everything [David] did he had great success, because the Lord was with him. When Saul saw how successful he was, he was afraid of him. But all Israel and Judah loved David.

(1 Samuel 18:12, 14–16)

2. A Tale of Two Paper Clips

The famous insurance company, Lloyd's of London, is known around the world for its policy of insuring almost anything and everything. Several actors, for example, have insured various body parts with Lloyd's. Singers have insured their voices. Athletes have insured their legs. Pee-wee Herman has insured his playhouse. If the price is right, Lloyd's of London has a policy to sell.

As you might imagine, to stay in business with that kind of special niche takes a huge amount of research in what insurance people call actuarial data—data that tells them whether or not they are likely to have to pay out on some policy they've written. Consequently, Lloyd's of London has one sector of its company that does nothing but research on almost every conceivable topic, ranging from what makes knuckles crack to whether winos are more likely to go bald than college professors.

One of their recent research projects caught my attention. I was astounded by what I found out. Lloyd's of London did some research in which they followed 100,000 paper clips to see how they were used. No doubt, this has been a question on the minds of many people. It's obviously time that someone gave us an answer to this vital issue.

What Lloyd's uncovered in their paper-clip study was shocking. Following 100,000 paper clips, they found that approximately 14,163 were bent and twisted during telephone conversations. Another 5,434 were used as toothpicks or ear scratchers (although the same paper clip was seldom used for both). Some 3,916 were used to clean pipes. An additional 5,308 were used to clean fingernails. A fairly large number—7,200—were used to hold together various pieces of clothing; and 19,143 were used as chips in card games. A full 25,000 fell ingloriously to the floor where they were swept away with the rest of the trash. (Shocking!) The real surprise was that only about 20,000 of the original 100,000 paper clips were ever used to clip paper together!

You're probably thinking, *This is fascinating!* And it is. I began with this exposé of the rise and fall of the paper clip because it represents a parable of life for a lot of us, a parable that teaches us a very important truth. If you think about it, the paper clip is a fairly remarkable creation. It is only one piece of wire bent and twisted three times. Yet nothing can do what a paper clip does as cheaply and efficiently as a paper clip.

Scripture teaches that each of us is a marvelous creation too. We are "fearfully and wonderfully made" (Psalm 139:14). God made each of us unique, in such a way that no other person on the planet has quite the combination of gifts and personality that each of us has. We were created with a grand design.

The tragedy is that out of 100,000 people created by God, a very small number of us ever go on to live up to the plan for which God created us. Far too many of us twiddle our lives away as toothpickers or earscratchers, just trying to hold things together or maybe getting swept along with the trash.

Two Paper Clips

In the following chapters we want to ask ourselves why some people really live lives that count for something while others more or less end up being just wasted paper clips. How is it that some people live up to the grand design for which they were created, and others end up getting swept along with the trash?

The Bible gives us a tale of two paper clips as we study the lives of Saul and David, two kings of Israel who lived about 1,100 years before Christ was born. Their stories are told side by side in Scripture, almost as if God wants us to compare and contrast the two men.

You've seen those commercials on TV that show us two products side by side. On the one hand is Brand Y, and on the other hand is Brand Y-Not. Typically, a hidden camera allows us to watch as someone tests the two products. Then, with complete sincerity, the person says something like, "I don't think this one tastes as good as Pepsi." And then, of course, the announcer says, "Yes sir, I'm sure that's true; but we're testing motor oil here."

It's that kind of comparison that God gives us in Scripture as we read through 1 Samuel 16:14-16:

> Now the Spirit of the Lord had departed from Saul, and an evil spirit from the Lord tormented him.
>
> Saul's attendants said to him, "See, an evil spirit from God is tormenting you. Let our lord command his servants here to search for someone who can play the harp. He will play when the evil spirit from God comes upon you, and you will feel better."
>
> So Saul said to his attendants, "Find someone who plays well and bring him to me."

Saul was no different from a lot of us. When we've had a lousy day at school, or an argument with a friend, we stagger through the front door of the house, go straight to our room, and turn on some tunes. Think about it: Don't you ever come home from school and say to yourself, *I've got to hear some harp music*? It's almost as if we want to get that music loud enough to drown out all the other voices that are screaming at us.

As it turns out, Saul's servants found just the man to be the king's musician.

> One of the servants answered, "I have seen a son of Jesse of Bethlehem who knows how to play the harp. He is a brave man and a warrior. He speaks well and is a fine-looking man. And the Lord is with him."
>
> Then Saul sent messengers to Jesse and said,

> "Send me your son David, who is with the sheep." So Jesse took a donkey loaded with bread, a skin of wine and a young goat and sent them with his son David to Saul.
>
> David came to Saul and entered his service. Saul liked him very much, and David became one of his armor-bearers. Then Saul sent word to Jesse, saying, "Allow David to remain in my service, for I am pleased with him."
>
> Whenever the spirit from God came upon Saul, David would take his harp and play. Then relief would come to Saul; he would feel better, and the evil spirit would leave him (1 Samuel 16:18-23).

David and Saul were a great team for a while. Saul went into moods of depression and started harping on something. Then, to keep him from getting too stressed out, his servants brought David in to start playing on the harp. It was a good match. Saul even promoted David to the position of being his personal armor-bearer.

A Bent Clip

Then came the episode with Goliath, the big Philistine bully who threatened to trample the people of Israel and wipe his feet on their God. Since Saul was their king and resident tall-person, the people of Israel looked to him to go out and meet Goliath in battle, to stand up to that loud-mouthed, pagan, strong man.

However, as you might imagine, Saul was not especially excited about an eyeball-to-kneecap wrestling match with an industrial-strength bad guy. When David volunteered to go out against Goliath, on what must have seemed like a suicide mission, Saul was only too happy to let his armor-bearer have the job. But when David actually won the showdown and slew the giant, he got the entire nation's admiring attention. That's when Saul's appreciation turned to jealousy.

> When the men were returning home after David had killed the Philistine, the women came out from all the towns of Israel to meet King Saul with singing and dancing. . . . As they danced, they sang: "Saul has slain his thousands, and David his tens of thousands."
>
> And from that time on Saul kept a jealous eye on David.
>
> The next day an evil spirit from God came forcefully upon Saul. He was prophesying in his house while David was playing the harp, as he usually did. Saul had a spear in his hand and he hurled it, saying to himself, "I'll pin David to the wall." But David eluded him twice. [Author's note: David was fortunate to be able to play and dance at the same time. In this sense, he was the father of modern rock and roll.]
>
> Saul was afraid of David, because the Lord was with David but had left Saul. So he sent David away from him and gave him command over a thousand men, and David led the troops in their campaigns. [Unfortunately for Saul, David's winning streak continued . . .] He had great success, because the Lord was with him. When Saul saw how successful he was, he was afraid of him. But all Israel and Judah loved David (1 Samuel 18:6-7, 9-16).

Comparing the Clips

In this passage, Scripture gives us a quick glimpse of two men, Saul and David. In some ways, they were very similar. Both men were great warriors. Both men were annointed and appointed by the Prophet Samuel to fulfill a special plan for God. And both men, in the course of their lifetimes, served as king for the people of Israel. But that's where the similarities end and the differences begin. That's where we begin to see the contrasts.

Saul's life was like the kind of clear summer mornings I remember growing up in North Carolina. Early in the morning, the sky was bright blue, sunny, and full of promise. But progressively throughout the day, the skies grew dark. And by nightfall, there were thunderheads on the horizon.

When it all began, Saul was a man with remarkable potential. He had everything going for him. But by the time we get to the last chapter of his life, this man—who had once been a brave warrior and charismatic king—was so fearful of going into battle that he first consulted with witches to see if he should fight. By the time the battle had ended, Saul was dead, pierced by his own sword in a final, suicidal act.

How did it all happen? How did one man with so much promise and so many gifts end up becoming just another wasted paper clip? How do you go from hero to zero in six chapters? In the next chapter, we'll take a look at the downfall of Saul.

3. The Downfall of Saul

Sometimes when I'm walking in the woods and see a fallen tree, I wonder how in the world anything that huge could be knocked down by a gust of wind or the weight of an icy coating. At one time it stood so tall, offering shade and protection for all that came under its branches. Now it lays there, brought low and broken, good for nothing but the fireplace.

Most of the time, if we take a careful look inside the tree, we will read a different story. A look beneath the bark shows years of rot, the scars of some disease, or the telltale dust of termites. As we look more closely, we begin to discover that it wasn't the gust of wind that made the tree fall. Rather, it was decay on the inside. The ice storm only exposed the rot that was there all along.

That's really the story of Saul: a tall tree in a forest of people. From all appearances, it looked like he would tower forever. But long before he crashed, the careful observer could begin to see him leaning. When he finally went down, it wasn't because of the fury of battle. The decay on the inside had started killing him long before.

It's a story all of us need to hear. It reminds us that no matter how much potential we show up front, there is no guarantee that we will continue to stand through the storm. It's amazing sometimes how the most gifted people, with every advantage and every sign of promise, can end up being wasted paper clips. And usually, it all begins with rot on the inside.

Step One: Saul Caves in to the Crowd

There were three key factors in the downfall of Saul. The first was that Saul caved in to the crowd. He took his eyes off the Lord and started trying to please men.

It all began when Saul faced one of his earliest tests as the young king of Israel. In 1 Samuel 13, we read that the people of Israel had faced off with their archenemies, the Philistines. The battle was nip and tuck, and the Philistines had moved into positions surrounding the Israelites. There they were, sandwiched on all sides by their enemies.

Then the Philistines decided to make the first move. They mustered their troops at Micmash. That shouldn't have surprised anybody. After all, if you have the enemy sandwiched, you're going to try to get your troops mustard (a little picnic humor). But, as you might guess, this really left Saul and his men in a pickle. Here they were, surrounded on all sides.

Not exactly the kind of situation you relish.

Even for a hot dog like Saul, it was clear this was no picnic. Some of his men wanted to run. They were saying (get ready for more picnic humor), "Lettuce leaf." But, of course, it would do no good to run because the Philistines would just (here we go again) "ketchup." On the other hand, they couldn't sit around on their buns. They had to do something, or at least it looked that way.

Before all of this mess began, God had given Israel strict instructions through the Prophet Samuel that her army should never go into battle without first offering a sacrifice. And no one should offer that sacrifice to God but His Prophet Samuel. That was the fly (another picnic reference) in this particular ointment. They were sandwiched by the Philistines, and Samuel had gone away for a period of seven days.

The situation became tenser and tenser. For seven days the people of Israel waited for Samuel's return, but it didn't look like he would get back in time to save them from defeat. By this time, morale was breaking down among the Israelite troops. Not only were they standing around knee deep in mustard, but some of Saul's men were beginning to dessert (the last of the picnic humor, I promise).

Finally, after waiting seven days—the time appointed by Samuel—Saul cracked. He caved in to the crowd and decided to offer his own sacrifice, with or without Samuel. "So he said, 'Bring me the burnt offering and the fellowship offerings.' And Saul offered up the burnt offering" (1 Samuel 13:9).

Then it happened. Just as he had finished making the offering, who should arrive back on the scene but the Prophet Samuel. And Samuel was ticked off:

" 'What have you done?' asked Samuel" (v. 11).

Between stutters and stammers, Saul came up with his excuse. (Read this with lots of feeling.)

> "When I saw that the men were scattering, and that you did not come at the set time, and that the Philistines were assembling at Micmash, I thought, 'Now the Philistines will come down against me at Gilgal, and I have not sought the Lord's favor.' So I felt compelled to offer the burnt offering" (vv. 11-12).

It was a great answer because Saul said two things that really sounded pretty good. First, he talked about seeking "the Lord's favor." That was a nice touch, and it sounded really spiritual. Second, he made it sound like it was everyone's fault but his own, that he was forced into this disobedience by pressure from the crowd. "*The men* were scattering . . . *You* did not come at the set time. . . . *The Philistines* were assembling at Micmash." Did you get all that? Saul was the innocent bystander: "I felt compelled to offer the burnt offering."

But Samuel shot right back through the smoke screen with words that must have stung the very heart of Saul: "You acted foolishly. . . . You have not kept the command the Lord your God gave you; if you had, He would have established your kingdom over Israel for all time. But now your kingdom will not endure" (vv. 13-14).

Lessons for Today

In looking at this passage, the first question I ask is: Why did Samuel get so frosted just because Saul offered the sacrifice? What's the big deal? Any of us might have done the same thing. After all, it seemed only reasonable.

I think most of us can imagine how Saul felt. God gives us clear guidelines about how we are to live our lives, how we need to obey Him with respect to our attitudes, our actions, our sexuality, our life goals. But sometimes those rules and principles don't seem reasonable. "Come on, God, You don't understand how much I love this guy." "Hey, Lord, You don't understand the way things are at my high school." "Lord, I can't afford to be giving a tenth of my income to the church. What am I going to buy clothes with?" Obedience in all of these areas doesn't seem to make sense sometimes.

But that's one of the lessons we learn from Saul's life: *Being reasonable is not the same thing as being obedient.* Saul had strict instructions from God that he was not to offer a sacrifice without Samuel, and he turned around and did just that. It was extremely reasonable, but it was wrong.

But couldn't he get partial credit? It's not as if he completely disobeyed God and went out and started fighting. He did, first of all, offer the sacrifice, didn't he?

Yes, but that's another lesson we learn from this passage: *Partial obedience is the same thing as disobedience.* Genuine obedience is not obeying God when we think it's reasonable and then ditching His guidance when we think it's unreasonable. God is looking for people who will trust Him, even in the heat of battle, even when it looks like it doesn't make sense, even when everybody else is saying, "Let's get out of town!"

And that's tough. Especially when our friends are putting the pressure on us. We expect the Philistines to reject God. But what are we supposed to do when some of our Christian friends are saying, "We've waited long enough; let's do it our way"? That's when the heat is on!

That day, encamped at Gilgal, Saul made a big mistake. He stopped listening to God and started listening to the crowd. He caved in to the pressure and did what was reasonable instead of what was righteous. Perhaps it didn't seem like so much at the time, but it was the first step to becoming a wasted paper clip.

For the second step in the downfall of Saul, let's go to chapter 4.

4. Religion as a Sin Screen

Those hot days in the desert must have been tough on Saul and his men. Yet the rays of the midday sun were nothing compared to the rage and heat that Saul felt from the Prophet Samuel.

Step Two: Saul Hides behind Religion

Saul was continually being burned for his unwillingness to obey God. That's what led him to the second step in his downfall: He started trying to cover up his disobedience by being religious. Unfortunately, he learned that phony religiosity doesn't make a very good sin screen.

> "When I saw that the men were scattering, and that you did not come at the set time, and that

> the Philistines were assembling at Micmash, I thought, 'Now the Philistines will come down against me at Gilgal, and I have not sought the Lord's favor.' So I felt compelled to offer the burnt offering" (1 Samuel 13:11-12).

You have to give Saul credit. He talked a good game. He was very careful to throw in just enough of the right words and phrases to sound like he was a very religious man. The next time you're in a tight spot because the principal caught you throwing food in the lunchroom or your parents caught you sneaking in late or the counselor at camp caught you sneaking out late, try this answer: "You know, I really wanted to seek the Lord in this thing. But I just felt compelled to take action." You never know; it might work.

Then, of course, Saul didn't charge into battle without first offering a sacrifice. He was smart enough not to disregard the instructions from God altogether. He was careful to first offer that burnt offering. It was almost as if Saul felt as if he could keep God off his back if he nodded in the direction of obedience. Maybe if he did some religious stuff like offering a sacrifice, Samuel wouldn't get so angry.

As it turned out, that was the second step in Saul's downfall. He never seemed to learn that *you can't cover up disobedience by being religious.*

There was another episode in 1 Samuel 15 when the same thing happened again. The army of Israel was once again embroiled in combat, this time fighting against the Amalekites (a tribe of people related to the Goflyakites). The Amalekites were a wicked people, and God wanted to punish them for the atrocities they had committed against His people, Israel. So He specifically instructed Saul to utterly destroy them: "Now go, attack the Amalekites and totally destroy everything that belongs to them. Do not spare them; put to death men and women, children and infants, cattle and sheep, camels and donkeys" (1 Samuel 15:3).

But what do you think happened? Did Saul do what God told him to do? No. Instead of doing what was *right,* he did what was *reasonable:*

> Saul and the army spared Agag [king of the Amalekites] and the best of the sheep and cattle, the fat calves and lambs—everything that was good. These they were unwilling to destroy completely, but everything that was despised and weak they totally destroyed (v. 9).

Once again, when Samuel confronted Saul, he got the same religious backpedal. Saul tried to cover his disobedience with religion: "The soldiers took sheep and cattle from the plunder, the best of what was devoted to God, *in order to sacrifice them to the Lord your God"* (v. 21).

"Come on, Samuel," Saul was saying, "you know we weren't going to keep any of that stuff. Yeah, honest. We were just collecting all of this great stuff so we could have an unbelievable campfire service tonight. Yeah, that's it. We were going to sacrifice all of this stuff to the Lord your God!"

But Samuel wasn't buying the act. Again, his rebuke was clear and cold: "You have rejected the word of the Lord, and the Lord has rejected you as king over Israel!" (v. 26)

If the Shoe Fits, Take It Out of Your Mouth

How often does something like that happen in our lives? We more or less do our own things. Then, when we get caught and the deal goes down, we end up putting a foot in our mouth by trying to cover up with religious acts.

There is a story told about two little boys. We'll call them Duffy and Guy. They were brothers. Guy was the older of the two. Their mother worked at their church as director of the kindergarten and day-care program. That meant there were occasionally days when they would be home alone after school without parental supervision. For Duffy, of course, this situation was no problem since he was exceptionally mature for his age. But for Guy, it represented some difficult temptations.

To make a long story short, one of those temptations involved their pet bird, Peepsie the parakeet. It was one of those days when Duffy and Guy were home alone after school that they started talking about how much Peepsie would probably like to get out and fly around like other birds. At the same time, they knew Peepsie would be unsafe if they let her go out into the wild blue yonder of their neighborhood. There had to be a safety plan.

Within half an hour, both boys were in the backyard tying a string to Peepsie's little feet so she could safely explore the yard. It seemed like the perfect idea—a living kite!

But, of course, boys will be boys, and they began to experiment with Peepsie, the living kite. How fast could she dive? How sharp could she corner? How fast could she fly around in a circle? It was that last question that really struck a chord. Before Duffy had a chance to stop him, Guy was swinging the bird through the air at somewhere around warp factor five. Instinctively, Peepsie had gone into a racing tuck, not even using her wings. It was quite a sight. (Of course, Duffy was disgusted by the whole business.)

It wasn't long after that when something strange happened. Peepsie stopped peeping. Her body went limp, and she stopped moving altogether. That's when they realized the tragedy: Peepsie had gone to that great bird cage in the sky.

The sound of the car pulling into the driveway broke the somber mood. Could it be their mom? The boys panicked. It was only a matter of moments before their mom was looking over the back fence as the boys walked toward the fence with Peepsie hanging from her safety line by the neck. Duffy was speechless. Guy, calling on all of his age and wisdom, knew exactly what to say. "Mom, guess what? The Lord called Peepsie home."

Even as Guy spoke the words, Duffy knew he was a genius. This was Guy's brightest hour. It sounded religious. It sounded thoughtful. It sounded good. But their mom wasn't fooled in the least!

We do that sometimes, don't we? We go through the whole week pretty much ignoring God or maybe only giving Him occasional obedience when it seems reasonable. Then finally, when another Sunday rolls around, we snap into our religious mode. We sing in youth choir. We take part in the worship service, or we go to youth group. And sometimes we even know how to talk the talk and throw in a few excellent religious-sounding words. But basically it's a cover-up.

God's challenge to us is the very same as His challenge to Saul: "Does the Lord delight in burnt offerings and sacrifices as much as in obeying the voice of the Lord? To obey is better than sacrifice" (1 Samuel 15:22).

In short, God says, "I don't want some phony religiosity; I want you. Involvement in the youth group, taking part in the work camp, and being in a small group is great. But don't let it become a substitute for obeying Me in the everyday affairs of your life. To obey Me is better than just being religious."

Some people never learn that lesson. Saul didn't, and he ended up becoming a wasted paper clip. Instead of honestly confessing his disobedience and turning his life around, he tried to play religious games with God. Sad to say, it didn't work.

5. If It's God, Tell Him I'm Not Home

In my high school biology class, we did an experiment to test an old hypothesis I had heard growing up. The hypothesis was that if you put a frog in a pan of water and slowly turn up the heat, the frog will stay in the pot until it is finally boiled to death. Fortunately, the biology teacher did not know we were doing this series of experiments. Even more fortunate was the fact that I had not brought Peepsie to school with me that day. We could have branched out in our research.

To our amazement, we watched as this huge frog, fully capable of springing from the pot, sat still in the ever-increasing heat of the water. As a cold-blooded animal, its system continued to adjust to the rising water temperature until finally it was too weak to save itself. It just sat there and died.

Essentially, that's what happened with Saul. Throughout Saul's reign as king with his frequent disobedience, God never stopped trying to get Saul's attention. God tried everything to convict and convince this guy that he needed to turn things around and start over again.

But Saul wouldn't listen.

Step Three: Saul Ignored the Spirit

The third and final step in Saul's downfall was that he continually ignored the Spirit of God.

Over and over again, particularly during the final years of Saul's reign, the Scriptures report that God was trying desperately to get Saul's attention, at times even tormenting him with conviction and depression (1 Samuel 16:23; 18:10; 19:9). And Saul felt the pressure. His moods ranged from guilt to fear to rage to jealousy. The torment was real.

At first, Saul tried to silence the gnawing conviction with music. The servants brought David in to play the harp, and for a while that seemed to help. But as time went on, it was clear that Saul needed more than some tunes. It became more and more obvious that the problem had nothing to do with the situation around him, and it had everything to do with the situation within him. The termites of guilt and the rot of fear had left Saul with some serious decay, feeling pain that could not have been silenced by an entire marching band of harp musicians.

What he needed to do was confess his sin and then start listening to God. But that wasn't Saul's way. He ignored the Spirit of God and sat there in the hot water. The worse it got, the more he seemed to adjust and tell himself, "This isn't so bad; I can take it." Finally, Saul—the man with unlimited potential—experienced a total spiritual meltdown. The King of Israel became just another wasted paper clip, fallen to the floor and swept away with the trash.

Society for the Preservation of Paper Clips

This section began with a comparison between two men, Saul and David. Now, the obvious question is this: Didn't David ever do anything wrong? Sure, he killed a giant here and there, but how about that business between David and Bathsheba? Didn't that get covered up somewhere along the way? What makes David so much better than Saul?

The answer is: nothing. David was no better than Saul. In fact, as we read David's story, we begin to discover that he was sinful in ways that Saul hadn't even dreamed of. David's sin went way beyond the burnt-offering level. During the course of his lifetime, David committed adultery, treachery, betrayal, murder, and more.

But there was one difference. When it all came out, David was willing to confess his sin and turn away from his disobedience. It took him a while, but he eventually came clean with God; and that action saved his life.

The fact of the matter is that David was no different from Saul at all. Neither am I, even as I write this book. And neither are you. That's why we need to take a look at Saul. What we're really doing is taking a look at ourselves.

We need to ask ourselves as we finish this chapter: Are there areas of our lives where we've caved in to pressure from the crowd? Have we opted for what seemed reasonable instead of doing what we know God tells us is right? Have we been honest with God about our disobedience, or have we been using some kind of religious "cosmetic" that makes us look more spiritual than we are? And finally, are we listening to God when He tries to speak to us? David was willing to listen to God. Saul tried to drown out God's voice.

The church is not a community of perfect people who never do wrong. The church is filled with both Sauls and Davids, paper clips that have been bent and twisted from all kinds of sin and disobedience. The difference lies in our willingness to respond when God tries to restore us to our original shapes.

There is nothing sadder than wasted potential—a paper clip that gets used as an ear-cleaner or a toothpick. Saul's story could be your story or my story. God has created every one of us with a grand design. It really comes down to our personal responses to Him. A few twists and turns the wrong way and a paper clip becomes just another piece of wire swept out with the trash.

Something to Think About

1. It must have been scary that day when Saul realized his army was surrounded by the Philistines. What do you suppose was going through Saul's mind? Do you think he was more concerned about the Philistines or about his own army and what they might think of him? Why?

2. One of the factors that seemed to trip up King Saul was the fact that disobedience often seems more

reasonable than obedience. A lot of times we find ourselves in those kinds of situations. What are some situations that you face on a weekly basis in which disobedience seems more reasonable than obedience?

3. For Saul, the pressure to disobey God came from two sources: the Philistines surrounding him and the Israelites standing with him. When, and with whom, do you really feel the pressure to disobey God's instructions?

4. God tried to get Saul's attention in different ways. He sent the Prophet Samuel to talk to him. He sent an evil spirit to torment him. What are some of the circumstances, and who are some of the people through whom God might be trying to talk to you?

5. Saul used music to drown out the voice of God. What are some of the other ways we try to drown out God's voice in our lives? Which ones do you use? Why?

SECTION TWO:
HOW GOD LOOKS AT PEOPLE

But the Lord said to Samuel, "Do not consider his appearance or his height, for I have rejected him. The Lord does not look at the things man looks at. Man looks at the outward appearance, but the Lord looks at the heart."

(1 Samuel 16:7)

6. Mr. Israel Contest

Do you ever talk to yourself when you're standing in front of the mirror in the morning? Most of us do. And we say all kinds of things. Some of us behold the spectacle facing us with pure admiration, absolutely stunned by the beauty of what we see. We just stand there saying to ourselves, "Oh, you animal. That face! That physique! That smile! Mirror, mirror on the wall, looking at me is such a ball!"

But for a lot of us, it's a completely different story. When we look in the mirror, we see things very differently. We're thinking that this person in the mirror has the nose of a parrot, the eyes of a lizard, the teeth of a beaver, and the complexion of a frog. When we stand there, saying to ourselves, "Oh, you animal," we don't mean it in any positive way!

Living Up to the Image

At first glance, David was one of those guys who didn't look like king material. He didn't really fit the mold. The Bible describes him as "ruddy [red-faced], with a fine appearance and handsome features" (1 Samuel 16:12). He wasn't a bad-looking guy. But he wasn't from a royal family. He was young. He'd been a shepherd most of his life. And, worst of all, his father Jesse was a grandson of Ruth, and Ruth was a Moabitess! (I hadn't wanted to mention this.)

"What is a Moabitess?" you ask. (Inquiring minds want to know.) Well, it sounds like a woman who goes around biting Moas, but it's not. A Moabitess was a woman from the tribe of Moab, and there were no foreigners more hated in Israel than Moabites. The very thought that their king had Moabite blood would have been disgusting to the people of Israel. It would have been like Hitler discovering that his grandmother was Jewish. It was just unthinkable.

David was as unlikely a candidate for King of Israel as you could find anywhere. He just didn't fit the part. When people were looking for a king in eleventh-century-B.C. Israel, the want ad did not read: "King Wanted: Should be young and inexperienced, ruddy in complexion, member of a bad family, and good with sheep." When David walked into the room, he wasn't the guy that inspired people to put their hands over their hearts and shout, "Long live the king!" More often than not, they put their hands over their noses and yelled, "Eeeecchh, clean that stuff off your shoes before you come in here."

A short look at David's long reign as king offers living proof that God's way of looking at people is much different from our own. We tend to judge ourselves and others by outward traits and external appearances. But God looks deeper than the hair style, the complexion, the family name, and the brand name.

A King Who Smells Funny

It was the eleventh century B.C. and Israel was getting restless. The people wanted a king like all the other nations around them. This business of having God as their leader was a little bit vague for their taste. They wanted a leader with flesh on his bones, someone they could look up to and bow down to. So the Lord raised up a man named Saul.

At first, Saul seemed like the perfect choice. He had everything going for him. He was a man of remarkable personal magnetism, genuine charisma, and natural leadership ability. And he was huge! The Bible tells us that he "stood head and shoulders above anyone else" (1 Samuel 10:23, TLB). It was obvious to everybody: Saul was Mr. It. He had it all.

But he was never really willing to give himself totally to God. He wasn't willing to put his throne under God's rule, and that attitude was his downfall.

It's a situation that reminds me of a car I used to have. It had a cool interior, a neat wooden dashboard with lots of toggle switches and stuff, an awesome radio that would play so loud it could make your eyes water and your ears bleed. And to dress it up, I covered the entire interior with shag carpet for that extra touch of elegance. (My dad made me take it off the windshield.) This car was a feast to the eye.

It only had one problem: It wouldn't run. I worked on it. I prayed for it. I sank money into it. But I could not keep that car running. It just sat there in the driveway looking good—great exterior, lousy motor. That turned out to be Saul's problem.

Finally, the situation became so bad that God decided to anoint a new king for Israel. That's where David entered the picture.

The Lord sent the Prophet Samuel to a man named Jesse, saying, "I have chosen one of his sons to be king" (1 Samuel 16:1). Samuel was to go to anoint (similar to a prayer of dedication) the new king of Israel. So far, that sounded simple enough. But it just so happened that Jesse had eight sons. Eight! We're talking Cinderella with seven sisters. So Samuel called them in one by one to see who was God's choice for Israel.

The first guy up to the plate was Eliab, the oldest of the sons of Jesse. He was probably a first-class stud, maybe a little bit cocky. No doubt he stepped confidently in front of Samuel with his hair brushed back, the gold necklace sparkling in the Mideastern sun, his shirt unbuttoned down to his navel: GQ meets Lawrence of Arabia.

At first, Samuel thought, "Great, this is him. The first one to bat and we already have a home run." But the Lord spoke a word of warning to Samuel, " 'Do not consider his appearance or his height, for I have rejected him. The Lord does not look at the things man looks at. Man looks at the outward appearance, but the Lord looks at the heart' " (v. 7).

Next up was Abinadab, the second oldest son and by far the one with the hokiest name. Again, another complete strike out: "Samuel said, 'The Lord has not chosen this one either' " (v. 8).

Then came Shammah, the next son. Again, no go. Then another son, and another, and another. Each of the seven sons passed in front of Samuel, but none of them got the nod.

Samuel, probably wondering if this was going to turn into some sort of wild king chase, asked Jesse, "Are these all the sons you have? No offense; they're good boys. But we came a long way out here to find a king, and we're going to be in deep trouble if we have to go back home without anointing somebody!"

After a long pause, Jesse reluctantly said, "Well, there is still the youngest. But he is out tending the sheep." What he was probably trying to say was, "Look, Samuel, you're really a great prophet, and I'm as into anointing kings as the next guy. But my boy David is not your man. He's great for shepherding sheep, but he doesn't seem like the type you would want shepherding people."

But Samuel insisted, "Send for him; we will not sit down until he arrives" (v. 11).

And sure enough, within a few minutes, everybody could smell David coming: royalty covered with sheep shoo shoo. He must have been quite a sight when he walked into the room.

Immediately, the Lord said to Samuel, "Rise and anoint him; he is the one" (v. 12). Thus began David's Cinderella story.

7. The Bible as a Mirror

The account of David's being anointed king of Israel is one of those rags-to-riches stories that everyone loves to hear. It makes you feel warm and fuzzy all over. But God doesn't give us His word to make us feel warm and fuzzy. He gives us His word so that we might better see ourselves and the God who made us. This Cinderella story in 1 Samuel 16 is no fairy tale. It's a story about folks like you and me.

To really understand what God wants to tell us from this episode, we need to ask ourselves two very important questions: (1) Why do most of us see ourselves as such losers when God looks at us with such promise? (2) What was it that God saw on the inside of David that told Him there's more to this guy than meets the nose?

How Do I Dislike Me?
Let Me Count the Ways. . . .

Why is it that most of us don't like ourselves? How is it that somewhere along the line we all got the idea that if we were one of Jesse's sons, he would have been introducing Samuel to the farm animals before he ever got around to thinking of someone like us? What is it that leads us to look at the image in the mirror and say, "There's no way God could do anything with a person like me"?

Competing with a Myth

One of the reasons we continually get distorted views of ourselves is that our major images of real humanity come through the media. It's subtle. We don't realize it. One weekend you end up at a Rambo or Rocky movie, and the next Monday morning you start to feel not quite dressed because your mom won't let you wear hand grenades to school. You begin to feel less than totally masculine if you aren't walking into the cafeteria, lifting up a lunch table, and yelling, "Yo, Adrian!"

It's often worse for girls. From your earliest days, you are given the subtle message that your only real value can be summed up in three measurements, none of which is an IQ. If you don't have a figure like Dolly Parton, a face like Michelle Pfeiffer, and hair like Cher, then you must have some sort of birth defect.

What are you supposed to think when, for the first 10 years of your life, you grew up playing with a Barbie doll, and now that you're 15, you begin to realize you don't really look too much like Barbie?

The problem, of course, is that in trying to live up

to these images, we are competing with a myth. It's like asking a real horse, "Why can't you be more like those nice horses on the merry-go-round? They're beautiful. They never get dirty. They never mess up the place. They never eat anything. They just bob up and down." Obviously, the answer is that those aren't real horses! The closer you get to a real horse, the more likely you are to discover some manure.

The front cover of the December 1990 issue of *Esquire Magazine* showed a beautiful picture of Michelle Pfeiffer with the story headline, "What Michelle Pfeiffer Needs. . . . " Most people would look at that cover and say, "Not a whole lot." That was what made it so interesting when Harper's Magazine published the bill that *Esquire* had received for the touch-up costs on Michelle's cover photo.

From Diane Scott Associates, Inc, in New York City, Esquire received the following item:

DATE	11 October 1990
CLIENT:	*Esquire*/T. Koppel
PRODUCT:	December Cover/Michelle Pfeiffer
DESCRIPTION:	Retouching 1 dye transfer two piece strip of Michelle Pfeiffer in red dress. Clean up complexion, soften eye lines, soften smile line, add color to lips, trim chin, remove neck lines, soften line under ear lobe, add highlights to earrings, add blush to cheek, clean up neck line, remove stray

	hair, remove hair strands on dress, adjust color and add hair on top of head, add dress on side to create better line, add dress on shoulder, clean up and smooth dress folds under arm and create one seam image on right side.
TOTAL	$1,525.00

And you wondered why your school picture didn't do you justice? We see these airbrushed, made-up images on TV, in movies, or in magazines and immediately begin to see them as the measure of completeness. We seek after their looks, their clothes, their style; and we measure ourselves by them. But we forget that, just like the merry-go-round, these images do not represent reality. They are meant only to provide entertainment. To compare ourselves to them is to compete with a myth. That is why some of the people who will read that article about Michelle Pfeiffer will struggle with bulemia and anorexia. It's tough to compete with a myth.

Packaging Is Everything

Another reason our self-images are distorted is because we live in America where packaging is everything. There is, in fact, a chain of stores in major cities with a catalog division named The Sharper Image. Think about that. I think they're trying to tell us and sell us something! We have becomc a culture that is obsessed with image.

I was speaking at a private school in Connecticut a few years ago. An attractive young girl came over to the table where I was having lunch with some students. The girl never spoke. She was introduced to me as Gucci Girl. Of course, we all chuckled. Then I asked why she was called that. Again, she didn't speak. She just smiled. She was very pretty.

Her friends responded, "Just look at her." And they began to go through her wardrobe item by item and point out the label and designer logo on each. They were right. This girl was a walking, talking—well, at least, walking—*Seventeen* cover.

I didn't think too much about it at the time. But later that afternoon, I got depressed thinking about that girl. Then it hit me: She's not really getting dressed every morning; she's getting decorated. She has become a showpiece, an object, a beautiful toy on the merry-go-round for people to look at and admire. The sad part, of course, is that no one ever develops a relationship with those merry-go-round figures. They get lots of admiration but not much love.

In our culture, it's very tempting to feel that we must "package" ourselves. If we make sure the label is right, nobody will care what's in the box. But that attitude tends to make us into beautiful, empty people—people who are so uptight about getting the packaging up to market standards that we are constantly discontent, unhappy, and ignoring those inner parts that make us truly human. That was the whole problem with King Saul: great packaging but no power. That is why God looks beyond the outward appearance. He looks for the inward heart.

Misunderstood Humility

Another reason some of us have distorted self-images is that we have a distorted view of pride, selfishness, and humility. Some of us have been raised to believe that the more we dislike ourselves, the more spiritual we are. I can still remember singing hymns that had lines like, "Would He devote that sacred head for such a worm as I?" and thinking how spiritual it would be if I could just consider myself a worm!

But I'm not so sure about that anymore. To begin with, I don't read in my Bible that Jesus died for worms. Years after that anointing episode in the house of Jesse, David reflected on why God would choose someone like him to do His work. What he painted was an altogether different picture:

> When I consider Your heavens, the work of Your fingers, the moon and the stars, which You have set in place, what is man that You are mindful of him, the son of man that You care for him? You made him a little lower than the heavenly beings and crowned him with glory and honor. You made him ruler over the works of Your hands; You put everything under his feet: all flocks and herds, and the beasts of the field, the birds of the air, and the fish of the sea, all that swim the paths of the seas (Psalm 8:3-8).

The phrase "heavenly beings" is the same Hebrew word as God. We are made a little less than God! How'd you like to have that written in your yearbook under your senior picture? If that's a worm, we're talking suuuuuperworm!

If God's view of us is so high and holy, where did we get the idea that it is spiritual to think of ourselves as jerks? It's largely because we have misunderstood the effects of sin. To really get the story straight again, we need to understand a few simple facts:

1. We have all been made in the image of God. We are holy and precious in His sight—even if we are overweight, need braces, have body odor, and flunk algebra.

2. Sin has marred God's image in us. The Bible says that we have not only been seeing the wrong image in the mirror, but we aren't even looking in the right mirror. The only real mirror that gives us a true reflection of ourselves is God's Word (James 1:22-25). We've chosen man-made images and man-made mirrors, and they have given us an untrue picture of ourselves.

3. Christ died for our sins so that He could restore us to the image of our Father, so that we could be like Him. But that hasn't completely happened yet. The mirror still looks out of focus at this point. But God is at work *in* us (Philippians 2:13). (He's not much interested in the packaging since He's not making toys.) And the image is getting clearer all the time.

So why did Jesus say, "If anyone would come after Me, he must deny himself" (Matthew 16:24)? He meant that we have to be willing to kill off the old images, put away the old identities and begin to set our sights on becoming like Christ. It doesn't mean that we hate ourselves, or that we try to kill off the unique parts of our personalities. And it certainly doesn't mean that I have to consider myself a worm!

What Does God See in David?

God didn't tell Samuel to anoint David that day because He just wanted to give the kid a break, because He champions the underdog (or the sheepdog), or because He thought of David as his personal "ruddy buddy." God saw some qualities in David that can't be photographed for a magazine cover or purchased at the mall. What God saw in David was unrelated to outward appearance. It had to do with his heart. And He's looking for the same qualities in us. To find out what they are, you'll have to read the next chapter.

8. A Great-Looking Heart

According to the Institute for Social Research, 3 percent of all Americans consider themselves to be handsome or beautiful, 26 percent consider themselves good-looking, 56 percent think of themselves as average, 13 percent judge themselves quite plain, and 2 percent see themselves as plain ugly. If in doubt, ask your friends which group you're in. I'm sure they'll be happy to tell you.

Usually, when we judge someone as ugly or attractive, there are standard physical features for which we look. Maybe it's the face. Maybe it's the legs. It could be the hair, the nose, the dimple, or various other points of interest.

But when God looks at us, what He looks at is the heart. Obviously, that doesn't mean God is literally doing some kind of spiritual electrocardiogram to see if Jesus is swimming in the aorta. Basically, when the Bible talks about our hearts, it refers to our attitudes, our mind-sets. Are we willing to hear God? Are we willing to obey God?

One lesson of Saul's downfall is that it takes more than good ears to hear the voice of God. It takes a heart that is willing to listen. When history told the story of Saul and David, the heart was the basic difference between the two men. David had a prepared heart.

What is a prepared heart? At first, it may sound like some sort of gourmet cannibal snack, but it's not. Basically, it's a *heart that is prepared to hear God and a will that is ready to obey God.* Jesus told a parable about different kinds of soil. One soil in particular was ready for seed. Consequently, the seed that fell on it "came up, grew and produced a crop, multiplying thirty, sixty, or even a hundred times" (Mark 4:1-20).

The seed is God's Word, and our hearts are the soil. Having prepared hearts means that we have allowed God to use certain events, Bible studies, people, and circumstances to prepare the soil of our hearts so that when He speaks, His seed will take root in our lives.

Tom was a great student in school. He came from an affluent Boston family and was headed for an Ivy-League education. Always decked out in the appropriate prep style, he was a sharp-looking guy on the outside. But in all the months he came to youth group, it seemed like there was nothing on the inside. No matter how many Bible studies, Sunday School classes, and retreats Tom attended it seemed like the seed was falling on rock-hard soil.

Dean, on the other hand, couldn't hear enough. Every week at Bible study, he was there ready to hear more, ready to try to make it a part of his everyday life. His heart was like fertile soil that had been carefully prepared for planting. As he heard new truth, it took root in his heart and began to bear fruit in the way he lived. That's a prepared heart.

Preparing a Heart That Hears

How can we have prepared hearts? We want to be all that we were created to be. We want to be sensitive to God's Spirit. But how do we develop those kinds of attitudes? How do we develop hearts that can hear? Here are some ideas:

Parents. Sometimes God uses the people in our families to prepare our hearts for Him. It may not always be pleasant, and it may not always be easy. But God can use parents to teach important lessons about obedience, trust, and unconditional love. David's parents, after all, named him Beloved. That says something about their commitment to their youngest son. They could have named him Whoops or Sheep Bait or something much worse.

Obviously, some people have parents who communicate less than unconditional love. That's sad, but it doesn't mean that God can't use those parents to teach important lessons about life, trust, and even forgiveness. It's not something we enjoy being reminded of, but God's preparation of hearts usually begins at home. Even when we get so mad at our parents that we'd like to put *them* on restriction or send *them* to *their* rooms, we need to realize that God's normal intention is to use these people to prepare our hearts for Him.

Friends. Sometimes God prepares us to hear His voice by speaking through our friends, teens in the youth group, or a youth sponsor. I can still remember the night I became a Christian. A high schooler named Donnie Selzer came over and said to me, "Well, Duff, what do you think about all this stuff?" It was the first time anyone my age had ever said anything to me about God, and the Lord used that one little sentence to get my attention.

That's one of the great advantages of having Christian friends. Sometimes God can speak through them to tell us something that we would never be willing to hear otherwise. I often wonder what might have happened if King Saul had known one friend like that—someone he really loved as a friend who was willing to talk straight with him about his downward slide.

Creation. One of the ways God probably prepared David's heart was by showing Himself through the majesty and wonder of His creation. I can remember a lot of nights backpacking with my youth group on the Appalachian Trail, sitting around the fire, and looking up into the nighttime sky when the number of stars was almost staggering. We couldn't help but marvel at the God who made them.

Remember that David spent most of his early years out under that same huge sky, watching his father's sheep. He knew that same sense of awe from looking up into the dark-blue canvas and wondering about what kind of God could paint this massive portrait of lights. In fact, it was David who wrote, "The heavens declare the glory of God," the skies "proclaim the work of His hands" (Psalm 19:1).

Next time you go skiing or surfing or hiking—or

watch a video of someone doing so—take a moment to think about the God who made that mountain, those waves, and the smallest fiber of tissue on the bark of those trees. Next time school gets cancelled because of snow, stop the celebration long enough to look out the window and realize that He made every single one of those snowflakes with a different design. No wonder David said, "O Lord, our Lord, how majestic is Your name in all the earth!" (Psalm 8:1)

Tough times. Sometimes God prepares our hearts to hear Him by allowing us to face tough times. Suffering is not one of those things we look forward to; but as C.S. Lewis put it in *The Problem of Pain,* "God whispers to us in our pleasures, speaks in our consciences, but shouts in our pains."

Chad was one of the guys in our youth group who usually felt comfortable talking about God. But you were never really sure how much he was actually talking to God. It probably wouldn't be accurate to say he was on fire for Jesus. It was more like a slow smolder.

He was popular at school, came from a great Christian home, had a good family situation, made decent grades, was a good athlete—Chad had it all. The only problem is, when everything's going that well, who needs God? Sometimes it's the Eliabs and Abinadabs with everything going for them (except their names) that have a tough time hearing what God wants them to do.

It wasn't until Chad was on a youth group mission trip to Haiti, sick in his room with dysentery and racked with pain, that he actually cried out to God. I'm not saying that God sent the bacteria that caused Chad's sickness just to get his attention. I don't believe that. But He does use situations like that to speak to us when He does get our attention. That bacteria wreaked havoc with Chad's stomach, but it did wonders for his heart.

The next time you go through a tough time or experience some pain or loss, try to take time to listen to God. Whether it's a friend moving away, the loss of a family member, or the pain of a broken relationship, try to listen to what God can teach you through the experience. It's not that God always causes these pains. The point is: He never wastes them (James 1:2-8).

The Bible. Probably the best way to allow God to prepare our hearts is by spending time in His Word. Assuming that most of us won't have a prophet drop by today, our best chance to hear God's call and His will for our lives is by studying Scripture. Judging from David's own writing, study of Scripture was one of the main ways God prepared his heart: "I meditate on Your precepts and consider Your ways" (Psalm 119:15).

The people I know who seem to genuinely have a heart for God are people who spend time studying the Bible. Sometimes that happens through a group study, sometimes it happens during the sermon, and sometimes it happens through personal quiet time. Usually, it happens through lots of different means. But getting in to the Word is a great way to open ourselves to the spade God uses to prepare the soil of the heart.

Reflections on That Face in the Mirror

Admit it. When you looked at that face in the mirror this morning and spent the next hour getting it ready, you weren't particularly consumed with getting your heart ready for school. That's understandable. It's the rare high school campus where a kid stops you in the hall and says, "I really like your ventricle."

There's nothing wrong with trying to look the best we can, but the heart should not be ignored. What is important is that we learn this key lesson from David's life: God sees not as man sees. *Man looks on the outward appearance, but God looks on the heart.*

David may not have been the coolest dresser, but he had designer genes. He had a heart that was willing to hear and obey the will of the Father. If we can blow off the propaganda that our culture gives us and keep David's perspective, God can do something incredible with our lives beyond our imaginations.

Something to Think About

1. God warned Samuel that the Lord does not look at the things man looks at (1 Samuel 16:7). What are some of the criteria with which man looks?

2. Why is it that we spend so much time dressing up the parts of our lives that God never really looks at?

3. In this chapter, we looked at different ways that God prepares our hearts. What are two recent examples of friendships or circumstances through which God spoke to you?

4. What are some ways that you can better allow God to prepare your heart for Him?

SECTION THREE:
HIDE-AND-SEEK—
THE STORY OF MEPHIBOSHETH

King David had [Mephibosheth] brought from Lo Debar, from the house of Makir son of Ammiel.

(2 Samuel 9:5)

9. Real-Life Hide-and-Seek

One of my favorite games to play with my children is hide-and-seek. I like it because I usually win. It was especially fun when they were little, before they knew how to walk. Then it was really easy. I would say, "OK, girls, count to a million, and Daddy will go hide." It gave me some time alone.

No matter how many times we play hide-and-seek, it seems like we always end up with the same basic pattern of pursuit. It usually begins with my girls saying, "You hide first, Daddy; we want to look for you."

So off I go to my favorite hiding place: the basement. I like hiding in our basement because it's a scary place. It's dark and damp and dank and dirty. There's also something sentimental about the place:

It reminds me of summers at church camp. Plus I've told my children that animals live in our basement.

After counting to five, they scream out, "Ready or not, here we come!" They immediately take their two-girl posse to the basement stairway. Then, standing there at the top of the stairs, they stare down into this frightening, dark abyss.

It's at that point that my oldest daughter, Erin, takes over. She's grown up around youth groups all her life so she fancies herself as savvy, hip, and street-wise.

She looks down into this dark basement and coolly decides to take action. She reaches over to the light switch; and with a triumph of nonchalance, she flips on the light.

But . . . it's still dark. That's because I have been to the fuse box and turned off the power in the basement! The darkness doesn't stop Erin though. Staring into this forbidding black hole of terror, she comes up with a scheme. She turns to her younger sister, Katie, and announces, "Katie, I have a plan. *You* go first."

With that, they start down the narrow stairway into the basement, moving slowly, cautiously, measuring every step. For me, this is always the funniest part of the game. If you've ever heard little girls sneak, it's a riot. First, there are giggles; then, a flurry of "Shhhhhh"; then, loud whispers and more giggles.

Finally, they reach the bottom of the stairway where they stop for a quick survey of the basement. That's when Inspector Erin takes over again. There is a large tool chest at the bottom of the stairs, tall enough for me to crouch in. It is just in front of where they are standing. Erin points to it and whispers, "He's in there." Katie giggles, nods, and giggles some more.

Once again, Erin has come up with a plan. "Katie, you open it." There's a barrage of whispered debate, and then it's decided. "We'll both open it."

Slowly, two little hands reach out to grab the doors of the tool chest. Shaky, tiny, sweaty hands move ever so slowly over to the doors until . . . *whoosh,* they jerk the doors open only to find . . . I'm not there! I never hide there because that's always the first place they look. Instead, I'm over on the other side of the basement hunkered down under a yellow workbench.

If you're a father, you have to make a strategic decision at this point in the game. If I keep hiding quietly, the girls will go back upstairs and leave me crouched in the dark. I don't want that to happen for two reasons. Number one, it is dark in our basement. Number two, there are animals that live in our basement.

So I choose to make a noise. Sometimes, I make the sound of a beating heart. Sometimes, I make a neat little sound like dripping water. Other times, if I'm really in a playful mood, I'll start up our chain saw. That tips them off.

Within seconds, I can hear them moving in the direction of the workbench, moving slowly again, cautiously, carefully. I can see them now: four skinny, white legs coming toward me in the dark. (One time I could have sworn I saw five legs; it scared me to death.) And then, just before they duck their heads down beneath the workbench, just when I see the little curls dip below the work surface, I reach out and grab their legs and scream!

"Ayyyeee . . . it's the bald monster! Run for your life." Little bodies fly in all directions, scared to death, yelling and laughing and screaming and running around. It's at that point that I keep telling myself that we have to put padding on those metal poles in our basement. The gongs of impact remind me of a human pinball game.

The scene is one of total panic. The kids are scared to death. I'm screaming. The kids are screaming. It's a riot. They are so terrified! In fact, their therapist has told us. . . .

Just kidding. It's all really a lot of fun.

Hide-and-Seek in Real Life

It wasn't fun, though, for Mephibosheth. Mephiphibosheth was playing a real-life game of hide-and-seek. There wasn't any laughter. There weren't any giggles. The stakes were very high. Mephibosheth's story is recorded in 2 Samuel 9.

> David asked, "Is there anyone still left of the house of Saul to whom I can show kindness for Jonathan's sake?"
>
> Now there was a servant of Saul's household named Ziba. They called him to appear before David, and the king said to him, "Are you Ziba?"
>
> "Your servant," he replied.
>
> The king asked, "Is there no one still left of the house of Saul to whom I can show God's kindness?"
>
> Ziba answered the king, "There is still a son of Jonathan; he is crippled in both feet."
>
> "Where is he?" the king asked.

> Ziba answered, "He is at the house of Makir son of Ammiel in Lo Debar."
>
> So King David had him brought from Lo Debar, from the house of Makir son of Ammiel" (vv. 1-5).

To understand this episode, we need to be introduced to the three main characters who walk onto the stage of the first verse in 2 Samuel 9.

One of the characters we meet in this episode is King Saul. He's dead by now, but as the first king of Israel, his presence still left a long shadow on the people of Israel. In many ways he was a great leader. In many others, he was weak-willed and double-minded. As we know, it was his unwillingness to sell out to God that left him tormented and defeated in the end, rejected by God as king of Israel.

It was Saul's rages and moods of despair that first brought him into contact with the second character. David was brought to the royal court because he was skilled in playing the harp and able to calm the royal temper tantrums with his music. Unfortunately, David turned out to be more than a good musician. He was also a brave and faithful warrior who came to fame in Israel after his showdown with the giant Goliath.

At that point, Saul began to consider David a rival and potential enemy. In fact, Saul's paranoia was so active that the Bible says, "From that time on Saul kept a jealous eye on David" (1 Samuel 18:9). Of course, if you've ever been in the library at school and laughed out loud at a friend's joke, you know what it means to eye someone. That's what the librarian does when she looks in your direction and gives you one of *those* stares where the eyes seem to burn a hole through the magazine you're hiding behind.

When you eye somebody, it's a way of saying, "You. I want you." One time when I was in junior high, Dad brought some business associates home for dinner. Mom had prepared a special spread for everybody. Thinking that the group might enjoy some after dinner humor, I commented, "Mom, this didn't taste much like pot roast. It tasted more like roast pot!" One guest laughed politely. Mom eyed me from that point on.

Saul's growing suspicion and increasing hatred of David made it especially difficult for the third character introduced in 2 Samuel 9. Jonathan was between a rock and a hard place because he was Saul's son and wanted to be loyal and faithful to his father. But he was also David's best friend, and he probably knew that David would and should someday be king of Israel.

So for Jonathan, the dilemma was clear. If he were going to be faithful to his father, he would have to be his best friend's mortal enemy. But if he were to remain loyal to his best friend, he would have to betray the father he loved. It wasn't an easy spot.

Finally, Jonathan and David met together in a secret meeting and made a vow to one another. Jonathan simply pledged that he would do all he could to warn David if and when his father ordered a plot for David's death. David, for his part, pledged that he would never cut off his loyalty to Jonathan and his family for as long as he lived, no matter what happened, no matter what it took to keep his promise.

It must have been a sad and dramatic meeting that

day when these two loyal friends embraced each other and wept that day in a field outside of the city. The two men never saw each other alive again.

Introducing Mephibosheth

A lot had happened by the time we get to 2 Samuel 9. Saul fell in battle at a little, out-of-the-way place called Mount Gilboa, the victim of his own sword. Killed at the same place was his son Jonathan, faithful to the end. So what happened in the opening verses of our story is that David asked around to find out if there was anyone left of Saul's household (and, therefore, of Jonathan's household) to whom he could show kindness for Jonathan's sake. He was trying to keep his promise of faithfulness to his friend who was dead but not forgotten.

That's when they brought in the old man Ziba (pronounced Zee-ba, like zebra without the r). Ziba was a great guy. He was easy to spot because he always wore a black and white striped robe (a little supposition). Ziba had been a servant in Saul's court so he knew as well as anyone if there were survivors from Saul's household. And, as it turns out, there was one.

Mephibosheth is one of those names that, as soon as you hear it, you begin to ask: Why in the world did his parents give this child a name like that? Other questions emerge as well. First of all, we want to know, Who was Mephibosheth? Secondly, Where was Mephibosheth? And thirdly, What was Mephibosheth?

The answer to the first question is easy. We read in 2 Samuel that Mephibosheth was the son of Jonathan, the grandson of Saul.

To really understand the second question, we need to know something about the way the throne changed hands back in those days. Unless the throne was passed down from father to son, becoming a king was usually a violent business. The normal policy of any new king was to completely wipe out all surviving family members of the preceding king as his first order of business. That would eliminate the threat of someone in the old regime coming back to reclaim the throne.

Mephibosheth had a funny name, but he wasn't stupid. He just assumed that when David became the new king, he and any surviving family members would be the first targets of a purge. Figuring that he was a fugitive from justice, he decided to put as much distance as he possibly could between him and the king. That's how he ended up in Lo Debar.

Lo Debar was a desolate little corner of the Mideastern desert in which Mephibosheth decided to spend his remaining days in a self-imposed exile. It wasn't exactly a garden spot. It was more like a sandbox with no walls and no toys. In fact, it was the pits.

How do I know it's the pits? Because Lo Debar comes from two Hebrew words which mean "no" and "place." That tells me the Chamber of Commerce was not very active in Lo Debar. You don't name your town No Place if you hope to attract tourists.

So there was Mephibosheth, holed up in the house of Makir the son of Ammiel in that out-of-the-way place called No Place. In modern language, we might call it No Man's Land. He must have figured it was the perfect place to hide from the king's terror.

That brings us to the third question, What was Mephibosheth? As if matters weren't grim enough, Mephibosheth was crippled in both feet. Apparently it happened when he was a little tyke. It was one of those occasions when they were evacuating the palace for fear that David and his army might launch an attack on Saul. The nurse carrying Mephibosheth dropped him as she hurried out of the palace and the fall crippled him for life.

Mephibosheth's story was not exactly a fairy tale. He had been exiled from his homeland, separated from his family and friends. He was lonely and scared, stuck out in the middle of nowhere, cornered in Lo Debar, cringing with fear, and crippled in both feet. That was the story of Mephibosheth—not exactly the kind of guy that someone would pursue for the sake of showing kindness. But then David didn't always operate by reasonable standards.

10. Choosing Lo Debar

I don't know about you, but I think that if I had been one of Mephibosheth's friends, I might have told him to give up, surrender to the king. No doubt he must have thought about it. How much worse could it be? He would either be a captive of the king or a prisoner of his fears. One way or the other, he was trapped. Why not just get it over with?

We can almost hear Mephibosheth rationalize with himself: *Lo Debar isn't so bad. It's quiet here. I have lots of time to think. . . . Of course, usually when I start thinking, I start thinking about David coming after me and how lonely I am out here. . . . But still, at least I know what I've got here. I don't know what might happen if I surrendered to the king. I know what I deserve from the king, and I sure don't want to face that.*

There is a sense in which most of us know exactly why Mephibosheth didn't turn himself in to the king. We can sympathize with his fear of the unknown. Most of us have felt it ourselves. We're willing to tolerate a lot of pain before we call the dentist, not because we enjoy decaying teeth but because we don't know what he might do. There's the fear of the unknown. Sure this is bad. Sure it hurts. But what might happen if I make the necessary decisions for change? That can be scary.

Caterpillars and Butterflies

I remember as a little boy, I used to enjoy playing with insects.

My favorite insect was the caterpillar. I used to love spending the day with one of those fuzzy little creatures. For one thing, they're versatile; you can do a lot of things with them.

For example, one of my favorite caterpillar games was to put one over my eye so that it looked like a huge hairy eyebrow. Then I winked at the little girls at the bus stop, and this huge eyebrow dropped off and hit my foot. It was classic.

Another time I brought a caterpillar home and draped him across my upper lip so that it looked like a big black mustache with an orange stripe. Then I strolled into the den and said to Mom, "Yo, Mom, guess who reached puberty today!"

I've always imagined that being a caterpillar is a bit of a bummer. For one thing, you have all these bratty kids doing gross tricks with you. For another, it must be tough knowing you have to go into a cocoon in a few weeks. That would be worrisome.

It's easy to imagine two caterpillars talking with

each other about whether or not they are going to report for cocoon:

"I'm not going."

"You have to go; everybody has to go. It won't be so bad."

"Oh, sure. Have you ever seen anybody come out? Noooo. What's going to happen to us in there? We don't really know. We might come out as anteaters!"

As a little boy, I used to imagine myself explaining to my caterpillar buddies why they should go ahead and hit the cocoon.

"Hey, why not? What's so great about being a caterpillar anyway? Think about it: You spend your entire day crawling around in the dirt, living in the mud, having people put you down and walk all over you. You call that a life? Why not just take your chances with the cocoon?"

Of course, caterpillars are suspicious little creatures. They're thinking, *Well, granted, this isn't much; but at least I know what I've got.*

"You see, you don't understand. You weren't meant to live like this. You weren't created to live your whole life down here in the dirt. You were made for more. You were created for flights above the treetops, feasting in the trees, and gliding among the flowers. None of this crawling garbage for you.

"You were meant to be an entirely new creature. You were meant to be a butterfly."

But the caterpillar would just shake his little head, "Ah, come on. You're just pulling my leg, pulling my leg, pulling my leg. . . . "

There is something in us that is very much like that caterpillar. We will tolerate all kinds of grief in the known because we're afraid to step into the unknown. We're like Mephibosheth in that respect. Maybe it *was* Lo Debar, but he was beginning to get used to it, and maybe he could make himself believe it was OK.

He Once Was Lost, but Now . . .

The day began like every other day at the house of Makir. Servants went about their work, sheep grazed, camels ate their hay, and Mephibosheth watched the horizon. It had become a ritual by now. Every new day brought the threat that the king would find him even way out in Lo Debar.

Perhaps it was in the middle of a long, hot, lonely afternoon that Mephibosheth heard the first shout from those along the wall of the compound. The announcement rang out, "Someone approaches from the distance!" Mephibosheth probably tried to shrug it off at first. *No worry. It's probably just a trading caravan or something. It'll be all right. They can't find me out here . . . can they? No, it couldn't be. . . .*

Then his thoughts were interrupted by a second word from the gate, "It's the king's chariots! It's the chariots of King David!"

We can only imagine what must have gone through Mephibosheth's mind at this point. First came the surge of adrenalin, then the wave of dread that crashed so heavily in his mind that he seriously thought for a fleeting moment about ending his life the way his grandfather had.

We can imagine this pathetic little man half crawling his way back into one of the inner rooms of the house. All the while, his mind raced with the realization that he had been found by his archenemy and should expect to pay the highest penalty for his rebellion. We can almost see this little clump of a man hiding under a table, beads of sweat rolling down his face, his heart pounding, his body heaving with fear.

Now he can hear the chariots as they enter the courtyard. Men shouting. Someone running. Just then the doors burst open. A shaft of daylight enters the room and standing only feet away from Mephibosheth is one of King David's stern-faced couriers. He barks his message: "Mephibosheth, King David wants you."

That ride back to Jerusalem must have seemed like it would take forever. Mephibosheth had ample time to consider all the ways that David might torture him and humiliate him. He had time to contemplate the exquisite pain that he would feel as he came under the whip of David's anger. Finally, after what seemed like an eternity, the chariot stopped at the palace and Mephibosheth was ushered into the throne room of his old enemy David.

We can only guess what the mood was in the throne room that day. It doesn't take much imagination to envision a mood of tension and quiet. Here was one of Israel's most wanted, an enemy of the king, being brought in for justice. My hunch is that when Mephibosheth approached the throne, perhaps dragging himself with his arms to the feet of David, there was a hush in the crowd. They expected the sentence to be quick, sure, and merciless.

That's why everybody was so shocked by what happened next:

> David said, "Mephibosheth!"
>
> "Your servant," he replied. [He was probably hoping in desperation to offer himself to David

> as a slave if only David would let him live. He could never have realized what would be David's next words.]
>
> "Don't be afraid," David said to him, "for I will surely show you kindness for the sake of your father Jonathan. I will restore to you all the land that belonged to your grandfather Saul, and you will always eat at my table" (2 Samuel 9:6-7).

At first, Mephibosheth must have thought it was some cruel joke, just one more wound to the spirit before David rendered the fatal wound to his body. Mephibosheth even asked, "What is your servant, that you should notice a dead dog like me?" (v. 8)

But it was no joke. "The king summoned Ziba, Saul's servant, and said to him, 'I have given your master's grandson everything that belonged to Saul and his family. . . . And Mephibosheth, grandson of your master, will always eat at my table' " (2 Samuel 9:9-10).

Mephibosheth the fugitive from Lo Debar had come home to become a member of the king's family from that day forward. The caterpillar with crippled feet began a new life of feasting at the king's table.

Although it happened 3,000 years ago, Mephibosheth's story is still being told even today. To find out why, turn to the next chapter.

11. Why Mephibosheth?

Mephibosheth is one of the unknown characters in Scripture. Guys like Noah, Moses, and Paul are the ones who have their robes hung in the Bible Hall of Fame. But few people have heard of Mephibosheth. To my knowledge, he hasn't achieved any flannelgraph exposure, and he certainly hasn't gained puppet status. So far as I know, neither Amy Grant nor Petra has written a song about the guy. (Granted, Mephibosheth is not one of those singable names that lends itself to a catchy tune.)

Yet his story is more familiar than many of us would like to admit. You see, there are Mephibosheths reading these words right now—folks who look like they've got it all together but are actually living right around the corner from Mephibosheth in their own private Lo Debars.

We don't like to admit it. Like Mephibosheth, we try to deny it. We try to rationalize away the loneliness, the fear, and the guilt. But we know they're there. Many of us turning these pages know the hurt of being separated from family and friends, feeling lonely and isolated, trapped by our situations, unable or unwilling to dig our way out.

Like Mephibosheth, we try to make the best of it. We tell ourselves that it isn't much, but it's what we know. We try to make peace with it and resign ourselves to living life in No Man's Land. Or we try to forget about it by partying, making big bucks, losing ourselves in a relationship, or burying ourselves in school work. But there's also that part of us that wonders about what is on the horizon.

Usually, those of us living in Lo Debar don't put much hope in God. If He's really there, we certainly can't imagine that He's looking for people like us for the purpose of showing kindness. We pretty much understand that we have rebelled against God and that all we really deserve is the strictest punishment.

Hunted by the Good Shepherd

That is why Mephibosheth's story is important for all of us today. God is a merciful King. And He is looking for us, not to stalk us and starve us and stick us, but to adopt us as His children. This God is not some bounty-hunting sheriff; He's a Good Shepherd who cares for and loves lost sheep.

It's true; we don't deserve it. The Bible says all of us have been crippled by a fall (Genesis 3:1-24; Romans 3:23). Every single one of us has rebelled against God's authority, whether in word, deed, attitude, or all of the above. And Scripture is just as clear that the penalty of sin is death (Romans 6:23).

The great news in this story, though, is that God loves us enough to come looking for us—not to harm us or hurt us but to hold us and help us. We were never created to live in the dirt and grime of a caterpillar lifestyle. God created us to be new creatures, freed from our sin, released from our Lo Debars, feasting in His presence.

The issue, of course, is our own response to this kind of love. Will we continue to run from it and hide out in our own private bunkers? Or will we accept Jesus' death on the cross as the payment of our own death penalty so that we can live in the presence of this loving King?

Running on Empty

I recently heard a true story about a woman who had the scare of her life. She was leaving a shopping mall. As she pulled out of the driveway, a trucker jerked his rig up close to her tail and started blinking the lights and blowing the horn. At first, the woman was embarrassed. She assumed that she had just pulled out in front of the truck, and now the trucker was giving her a dose of rebuke. But as they pulled out of the mall parking lot with the trucker tight on her bumper, her embarrassment turned to anger. *The nerve of this guy,* she thought.

As she accelerated through traffic, trying to pull away, she was shocked to see the same truck grill in her rearview mirror, still with lights blinking and horn blowing. Now her anger was mixed with a hint of fear. Maybe this guy was going to offer his rebuke in a more violent way. She began to drive even faster, searching for her exit, keeping one eye on the rear-view mirror. Despite some very tight cuts through traffic, the truck was still right on her bumper.

By the time she cut to her exit, the trucker barely had time to rip his load across two lanes, air brakes hissing as he followed her down the exit ramp. She ran the light, and he followed her through. Now it was no longer anger or fear she was feeling. It was sheer panic. By the time she screeched to a stop in front of her house, she was terrified.

As the truck ground to a halt just behind her car, she swung the door open and started running for her house. The door of the truck flew open as well, and the driver was also off at a dead sprint . . . except he was running in the direction of the woman's car. The woman stopped on her porch long enough to look back and see the truck driver open the door of her car and lunge into the back at a man holding a knife.

Apparently the truck driver had spotted this man hiding in the woman's car back at the shopping mall. He had tried to get her attention so she would abandon her car and move to safety, but she didn't understand. She thought the trucker was out to hurt her. As a result, she had been trying to outrun a man who only wanted to save her life.

It's possible that this same drama is being played out in your life, or in the life of a friend, as you read this book. It's quite possible that a lot of us are running and hiding, hoping to escape a God who only wants to save us and embrace us.

"Hey, It's Only Dad!"

When I play those great games of hide-and-seek with my daughters, the best part is when they lose.

First I come screaming out of the darkness; and they freak out, running all over the place. Then, after about ten steps, Erin, the older one, turns back to look at me; and she freezes. She looks at Katie, looks at me, looks at Katie. And then she says, "Hey, we don't have to be afraid of him. That's Daddy. Attack!"

All of a sudden, the three of us are rolling around on the floor of the basement, laughing with each other, tickling each other, and hugging each other. It's a party because they realize they don't have to be afraid of me. I'm their Dad.

This may sound weird, but if you're beginning to recognize Lo Debar as somewhere in your neighborhood, I want to invite you right now to come out of hiding. We don't need to be staggering around in the dark, hoping like crazy we'll find God but scared to death He might find us. He loves us. He's our Dad!

I don't know what your father is like here on earth. But I do know your Father in heaven. Believe me, even today He is looking and longing for fugitives from Lo Debar. If you've never made any kind of commitment to Him, I want to invite you to pray the prayer below. It's a prayer of surrender to the King of all kings and a way of saying to God that you're ready to come out of hiding.

> Father in heaven, I know I'm a rebel, a sinner who has chosen to go his own way rather than give myself to You. But, Lord, I'm tired of trying to pretend that Lo Debar is where it's at when I know that Lo Debar is where it isn't.
>
> I am thankful, Lord, that You sent Your Son Jesus to die on a cross, to pay the debt of death that I rightfully owe. I thank You as well, Lord,

that this same Jesus rose from the dead, and invites me to live each day with Him in Your presence.

I want to come out of hiding, Lord, and live my life for You. I know I don't deserve any of this, that it's all by Your grace and love. My Father and King, I want to be Your servant from here on out.

I pray this in the name of Jesus. Amen.

Something to Think About

1. What are some of the ways you personally feel trapped? What kind of Lo Debars are you facing right now?

2. What are some of the ways we try to rationalize away the pain of our Lo Debars? In what ways do you try to hide from some of the guilt and hurts with which you deal?

3. What are some of the reasons we choose to stay in our Lo Debars? What are some of the factors that keep us in hiding?

4. Why do you think so many of us think of God as the Good Sheriff instead of the Good Shepherd?

SECTION FOUR:
ANATOMY OF A SIN

Now a traveler came to the rich man, but the rich man refrained from taking one of his own sheep or cattle to prepare a meal for the traveler who had come to him. Instead, he took the ewe lamb that belonged to the poor man and prepared it for the one who had come to him.

David burned with anger against the man and said to Nathan, "As surely as the Lord lives, the man who did this deserves to die!"

Then Nathan said to David, "You are the man!"

Then David said to Nathan, "I have sinned against the Lord."

(2 Samuel 12:4-5, 7, 13)

12. A Traveler Visits the King

Aaron Burr was one of those guys you heard about in history class, but you never felt like you were getting the whole story. You remember Aaron Burr. He made his niche in history by taking part in a pistol duel with Alexander Hamilton, a duel in which, unfortunately, Hamilton came in a poor second. I can still remember that every time I heard that story, it just never sounded right to me. I knew there must be more to it. I had a strong hunch that Mrs. Turbeyfield was protecting our second-grade class from some messy business.

Was that ever true! This guy was incredible. Aaron Burr makes The Joker look like a choir boy. We're talking about the only U.S. Vice-President to preside over the Senate while under indictment for murder, and the only ex-Vice-President to be tried for treason. In short, Burr was a very heavy dude.

Apparently, the boy had a weakness for widows because he was constantly getting involved with someone whose husband had recently died. His first wife, Theodosia, a New Jersey girl, had been married to a British army officer who was away on duty in Jamaica. That's when she met Burr and began spending time with him. When her husband died from a fever while on duty in the West Indies, Theodosia promptly turned around and married the young, soon-to-be lawyer Burr.

That relationship ended abruptly after only a few years when Theodosia developed a serious illness. It wasn't the sickness that killed her though. It was the hemlock prescribed by Dr. Benjamin Rush, a well-known Philadelphia doctor. That left Burr a thirty-eight-year-old widower with a ten-year-old daughter.

As a widower, Burr renewed his relationship with one of his earlier flames, a Philadelphia socialite named Rebecca Smith. Unfortunately, in the years since their initial relationship, Rebecca had married a man named Samuel Blodgett, Jr. Shortly after Rebecca and Aaron started seeing each other, it happened again. Blodgett died and named Burr the trustee of his estate including, of course, his dear wife Rebecca.

Then along came another friendly widow, Mrs. Dorothea Todd, who mysteriously named Burr the sole guardian of her young son. Interestingly enough, Burr fixed her up with his friend James; and she later became Mrs. James (aka Dolley) Madison.

In 1800 Burr took some time away from his ministry to widows to make a run for the presidency. In that race, he tied with Thomas Jefferson; but by a

House of Representatives vote was elected Vice-President. That action put Aaron in a very testy mood. It was in that mood that he challenged his political archrival Alexander Hamilton to a duel. As a result of his very strong showing in that duel, Burr found himself wanted for murder in two states.

That's when he decided to stay out of sight for a while. Eventually, his travels took him to New Orleans where he befriended Mr. and Mrs. Blennerhasset, who happened to be uncle and niece as well as husband and wife. At some point during this time, while Burr was knocking around in New Orleans, he: (1) attempted to start a separate empire from the Louisiana Purchase; and (2) contacted Napoleon about the feasibility of an attack on Boston.

Burr had one last disastrous fling in his sunset years with Mrs. Elizabeth Jumel, whose husband Stephen died when he fell off the back of a wagon on a New York street. Elizabeth and Aaron shared one year of wedded bliss before she filed for divorce, accusing Burr of numerous affairs.

The story goes on, but you get the idea. It was not a happy chapter in American politics. The irony of it all is that Aaron Burr was—get this—a preacher's kid. In fact, he wasn't just any preacher's kid. His grandfather was Jonathan Edwards, the pastor of the church in which this country's most significant, nationwide revival began. What has become known as the Great Awakening began in the church pastored by Burr's granddad!

Just Another Crooked Politician

Nowadays we're used to stories of crooked and corrupt politicians. We're just as apt to read about a political leader in the *National Enquirer* as in *Newsweek.* But the gory details of a life like Aaron Burr's still leave us with a sense of shock and disbelief.

What is even more disappointing, though, is when we read those same kinds of stories about well-known Christian leaders who have been caught (so to speak) with their hands in the cookie jar. Even in a culture where sin is as common as air, we somehow expect our Christian leaders to keep their heads above the murky water. We feel a special sense of confusion and hurt when they start to sink.

I guess that's why I've always been so amazed with the way the Bible portrays its heroes. We might have expected the biblical authors to clean up the stories a bit before they went to press—maybe change a few things here and shade a few things there. We're a little surprised to see some of the Bible's greatest saints involved in episodes of drunkenness, incest, deceit, murder, jealousy, and more. This is not exactly what we learned from the flannelgraph stories in vacation Bible school. (If it had been, we might have been more eager to come!)

Alexander the Great once had a portrait painted of himself in which his face was posed in his hands as if he were deep in thought. In fact, the Great One chose the pose because he wanted to cover up an ugly facial scar he had received from a battle wound. The Bible includes no such cover-ups. What you see is what you get. The Bible gives us both saints and sinners, warts and all. There's no apparent attempt to make it tidy. In fact, maybe one of the greatest proofs of the Bible's reliability is the uncanny honesty with which it portrays even its heroes.

A Beloved King, a Beautiful Woman, and an Ugly Story

When it started off that day, it probably didn't seem like an ugly story was unfolding. In fact, on the face of it, no one would have guessed that this was the first chapter of the greatest tragedy in David's life. It all began innocently enough on a spring afternoon with David strolling on the roof of his palace.

> From the roof he saw a woman bathing. The woman was very beautiful, and David sent someone to find out about her. The man said, "Isn't this Bathsheba, the daughter of Eliam and the wife of Uriah the Hittite?" Then David sent messengers to get her. She came to him, and he slept with her. . . . Then she went back home. The woman conceived and sent word to David, saying, "I am pregnant" (2 Samuel 11:2-5).

In that short episode were the seeds of unbelievable pain, tragedy, and suffering. It's a story that has been told over and over again through time, and its plot is as fresh and familiar as the temptations you face this week. We want to look at this episode more closely to see if we can learn something about the anatomy of sin: how it's born, how it's built, and how it bowls over everybody in its path.

Lesson Number One: Sin Is Sneaky

I used to love riding in the car with my youth group kids after they had just gotten their driver's licenses. It was great because they were so incredibly cautious. First there's a check to the left, then a check to the right, a check of the five-day forecast, a review of all hand signals, a glance at all gauges, a readjustment of all mirrors. Then maybe, just maybe, after a word of prayer, they might be ready to start the ignition!

Three years later, though, watch out. Now this kid's an experienced driver. He knows the roads, and he doesn't need all that drivers ed. propaganda. This same kid who was Mr. Safety, Junior Highway Patrolman, and Officer Friendly all rolled into one is now a terror on wheels! He only adjusts the mirror so he can fix his hair. The only hand signals he uses are directed at other drivers who get in the way. The only gauge that matters reads AM and FM. That's when he starts to get careless.

King David was in that same high-speed, cruise mode when he went into the skid with Bathsheba. He was moving forward, making good time, and starting to get careless. That's when sin knocked him off the track.

Early in David's reign as king of Israel, his rule was marked by a sensitivity to the direction of God. He was cautious to go when God said go, and stop when God said no. His campaigns were orchestrated under the guidance of God. His armies fought with the blessing of God. His nation seemed to be focused on the worship of God. It was a heady time for David and the people of Israel. You have to wonder if all of that success didn't begin to lull David off his guard and lead him to figure he could coast for a while.

Beware the Wandering Traveler

When Nathan the prophet later referred to this Bathsheba scandal, he called David's rooftop temptation that day a "traveler," almost like the proverbial accident looking for a place to happen. What it really turned out to be was a "look" accidentally happening in the wrong place. It was a temptation that snuck up on David's blind side and nailed him with a direct hit. Unfortunately, that's usually the way sin works. It sneaks up on us and throws the sucker punch.

After David showed kindness to Mephibosheth, he led his troops in a series of successful battles with all comers. There were the Arameans, the Moabites, the Edomites, the Ammonites, the Jeddi Knights. (I got carried away with the list.) One after another, they fled in the face of Israel's army. David's throne was strong and secure.

As chapter 11 opens, David was pacing the palace roof and savoring his recent victories. His army was out on some mop-up maneuvers at an Ammonite stronghold in Rabbah. "But David remained in Jerusalem" (v. 1). His men were in the field, but David was on the rooftop. Literally and figuratively, David was standing tall. The situation seemed to whisper, "Watch out, David, your guard is down."

So often that is the case, isn't it? Our greatest temptations come just after our greatest victories. Like when you finally learned to ski, and you made it all the way down the chair lift ramp without falling. So you figured, *No problem. I'm ready for the black diamond slope now.* The guard is down, the pride is up, and you're headed for a fall! The humility and caution that allowed you to succeed in the first place is pushed into the background by your accomplishments.

Satan is smart. He sneaks up on us in our moments of highest highs and lowest lows when we're distracted by other matters. It's not usually the direct frontal assault. Instead it normally begins with some innocent situation, a temptation that comes to the door as a wandering traveler.

My friend Danny learned this lesson the hard way. Coming back from a Young Life camp weekend, he was pumped. He had made a commitment to Christ over the weekend and couldn't wait to get back home and begin to share his new discovery with his family. Unfortunately, when he got back home, he returned to the same old family situation—an abusive alcoholic father and a mother who was never home because she had to support the family. Coming off of the spiritual high of the weekend, it was a long drop for Danny; he fell hard. He hadn't been home 48 hours before he got into a fist fight with his dad and ended up running away from home.

For Jan, it was a different story. The school year had ended, and she was getting ready to go away for the summer. Through a chance meeting, she ran into one of the guys from the youth group; and they started talking. As the conversation went on, Dean suggested they go back to his place where they could be more comfortable. When she shared the incident with me later, she said it seemed only natural that they held each other close as they spent some time in prayer. Neither of them expected anything to happen. But when the clothes started coming off and the praying stopped, it didn't seem so innocent anymore.

There are really only two good ways to avoid temptation. One is to *stay on guard.* Don't allow yourself to be put in a situation that is going to open you to an attack. Sometimes we allow ourselves to get in situations where we might as well wear a sign that reads: "Visiting Hours. Wandering Travelers Welcome."

You know what those situations are for you. As we learn from David's story, inviting a nude woman over to your house for a chat after her bath would probably fall into this category.

For other people, the off-guard situation might be a time of depression. Or it might be when they're around a certain group of friends or when they go to a party. Or it might just be when they're alone. It's going to be different for all of us.

The point is that no matter how long we've been Christians, no matter how strong we feel we are in our walk with Christ, we can't afford to be careless. We need to stay on guard. As Peter put it, "Be self-controlled and alert. Your enemy the devil prowls around like a roaring lion looking for someone to devour" (1 Peter 5:8). When we start hanging around, savoring the victories, we better be careful that we're not cruising for defeat.

The other way to avoid temptation is to *keep moving forward in your walk with Christ.* Never become too satisfied with where you are in your commitment. We will never be so spiritual, so totally together, or so completely in touch with God that we can afford to stop moving forward, claiming new ground in our relationship with Jesus. In the Christian life, there's no such thing as neutral. The day we stop moving forward is the day we start falling backward.

That's one of the reasons that it's always a good idea to have a plan of action when you return from a camp or a retreat. Before you return home, plan how you're going to continue to maintain the spiritual ground you gained while you were on the trip and how you're going to continue to seek new areas of growth. The guy that discipled me put it this way: A success not followed by a process often becomes an abscess.

When God gives you some new insights—any time you gain some new spiritual ground—plan ahead about how to cultivate that commitment. Always keep moving forward in your spiritual life. Otherwise, what could have been a milestone of growth may become a tombstone of failure.

13. How to Sin: Five Easy Steps

How often do you wake up in the morning and think, *I guess I'll sin today?* To be honest, most of us don't plan to sin. Instead, we're drawn into it gradually, just like David.

Lesson Number Two: Sin Is a Process

The second clear lesson that we learn from David's adulterous affair with Bathsheba is the fact that sin is a process. Most of us don't fall with just one huge jump of disobedience. More often than not, it's a slow descent with many smaller steps.

David never went to the roof of his palace that day with plans to commit some major sins. He didn't go up to the rooftop that spring afternoon to see if he could spot any women bathing. When he saw Bathsheba, he didn't swoop down on her from the roof of the palace and rape her. David did not jump into sin; he slid into it.

If we think about that episode, we can begin to catch glimpses of the downward slide. Read back through the first five verses of 2 Samuel 11 and underline the verbs. The plot goes like this: David remained at home; he saw a woman bathing; he inquired about her; he sent messengers to get her; he slept with her.

Temptation is like any other seedling. If it's plucked out of the ground early enough, it won't bear any fruit. But if it's allowed to grow, it becomes prominent and productive. Eventually it will bear the fruit of some sinful action or attitude. Let's walk through the process of David's slide so we can learn to deal with the temptations we face on a daily basis.

Step One: He Remained in Jerusalem

My mom used to say that "an idle mind is a devil's workshop." There's some truth to that. If David had been out on the front with his troops, he wouldn't have been home that day when the "wandering traveler" stopped by. The best way to keep temptation from blossoming in our lives is to stay out of areas where the seeds are being sown.

Most of us know our weak areas. The problem is that we don't know them as well as we think we do. We think we're good drivers until we get into a wreck. By then, the damage has been done. The smart thing to do is avoid situations that will make you vulnerable to temptation. For example, when the Pharaoh's wife tried to seduce Joseph, he didn't mess around; he just took off (Genesis 39). Scripture even says, "She caught him by his cloak and said, 'Come to bed with me!' But he left his cloak in her hand and ran out of the house" (v. 12). Better to lose a good coat than a good conscience.

Step Two: He Saw

Remember that Sunday School song: "Be careful little eyes what you see"? That's sound advice. One of the major ways temptation enters our awareness is through the eye gate—especially for men. We can be in biology lab, see two fruit flies mating, and we get all hot and excited. Sin first entered into the world "when the woman *saw* that the fruit of the tree [of the knowledge of good and evil] was good for food and *pleasing to the eye*" (Genesis 3:6, italics mine).

So what can we do? We can be careful not to spend a lot of time looking at forbidden fruit, whether it's on the test paper on the next desk over, or on the screen of the television, or on the posters in our rooms, or on the hunk that just walked by in the hallway. It's not that seeing is a sin; it's that temptation often comes to us through what we see. That's where we need to be smart and use caution. When David ordered his servants to break out the royal binoculars, he had already started the slippery slide into sin.

Step Three: He Investigated

This is when David really started playing with fire. The best way to avoid sin is to flee from temptation. Instead, David invited her over to his house! We're only kidding ourselves if we go this far in the slide to sin. It gets real slippery from this point on.

There is something about our nature that makes us

want to see how far we can go and still step back just in time. So we test, we inquire, we investigate, and we glance. But if we're really serious about playing it safe, we're not going to see how close we can get to the edge without going over. Instead, we're going to stay as far from the edge as we can.

We rationalize: "But I just want to know for myself." "I'm not going to get involved with this stuff." "I'm just experimenting." "I just wanted to know what it was like. I wasn't going to do anything wrong." It reminds me of the preacher who was ranting about an X-rated movie in town and said, "Brothers and sisters, by the time I sat through that trash four times, I knew I had to preach against this filth!"

Step Four: He Planned

We don't really know at what point David made the shift from flirting with temptation to planning to sin. If we had asked David later on, even he might not have been able to answer that question. By the time David sent messengers to bring Bathsheba back to the palace, he probably knew it was going to be more than just a friendly chat with his neighbor.

I went through a brief period in elementary school when I was into carnivorous plants. Those are the plants that eat living insects like houseflies, gnats, and moths. I had a small collection that included three different species. I spent rainy afternoons catching flies, putting them in between the leaves, and then watching them squirm as the leaves began to close. I started to get bored with this routine after a while and eventually ruined my plants by trying to feed them other foods: ants, earthworms, jello, jelly beans.

When I look at David's slide into sin and think about how many of us follow that same slippery route, I'm reminded of my trumpet plant. I remember how it would entice flies over to its funnel-shaped stem with its sticky liquid. Flies would get in there and move closer and closer, deeper and deeper, thinking, *This is incredible. What a feast. I must remember the name of this place so I can recommend it.* The next thing they knew, they were stuck. They couldn't get out. Within an hour they were dead.

Sin can be like that. We get closer and closer to the edge, thinking we can pull out, until something in us just surrenders to the temptation. Then it's too late. I think the key is not to trust our hearts to guide us but to realize there is a point when emotions overrule the brain. "The heart is deceitful above all things and beyond cure. Who can understand it?" (Jeremiah 17:9) The best way to avoid that long fall is to set some solid convictions beforehand—guidelines and safety lines that can keep us back from the edge when the heart says, "Go for it."

Step Five: He Acted

Up until this point, David still could have stopped this mess. There is no such thing as the devil making us do it. Sin is an act of the will. If we really want to resist temptation, God will enable us to do so:

> No temptation has seized you except what is common to man. And God is faithful; He will not let you be tempted beyond what you can bear. But when you are tempted, He will also provide a way out so that you can stand up under it" (1 Corinthians 10:13).

Unfortunately, David acted. And every action has a reaction. For David, the consequences of his decision to sin were far-reaching and long-lasting.

14. Fatal Attraction

When David fell into adultery, there is every reason to believe he thought that one brief afternoon fling would be the end of it. It would be one of those quick deals that no one would know about. Then he could quickly shift back into gear being a man after God's own heart. It wasn't like he was totally dumping his commitment. This was only one time with only one woman. Just like in the movies, it would be spontaneous and uncomplicated.

Lesson Number Three: Sin Attracts More Sin

Unfortunately, David could not have been more wrong. The third lesson we learn about sin from this situation is that the main result of sin is almost always more sin.

The first complicating factor in this messy business was the fact that Bathsheba became pregnant. That made everything a bit more difficult. To begin with, there was the question of her husband Uriah. He was out on the battlefield with David's troops at this point, but he would eventually return home. He might notice that there was a new son around the house and that he had not been home in the last nine months to help conceive him. He could begin to get suspicious. So David began to formulate a cover-up scheme.

It would be simple enough. He would immediately send word to Uriah that he should come back to Jerusalem for some R & R. Uriah would come back from the front and enjoy a few days at home, during which he would, no doubt, sleep with his lovely wife. That way, when the child was born, he would just assume it was his own.

But the plan backfired. What David had not counted on was Uriah's devoted faithfulness to his duty and to his troops in the field. Although Uriah returned to Jerusalem as ordered, he refused to go home and be with his wife. He simply didn't feel it was right for him to be there enjoying his warm home and beautiful wife when the other guys were still out in the battlefield:

> Uriah said to David, "The ark and Israel and Judah are staying in tents, and my master Joab and my lord's men are camped in the open fields. How could I go to my house and eat and drink and lie with my wife? As surely as you live, I will not do such a thing!" (2 Samuel 11:11)

David even invited Uriah over to the palace so they could drink and swap war stories, hoping that he might get Uriah drunk enough to betray his conscience and go home to his wife. But Uriah wouldn't do it. He chose to bed down with the servants rather than go to his own home.

That's when David realized he would have to take more desperate measures. The next morning, he wrote a letter to Uriah's commanding officer, Joab, with very specific instructions: "Put Uriah in the front line where the fighting is fiercest. Then withdraw from him so he will be struck down and die" (v. 15).

This time David's schemes accomplished his goals. Joab placed Uriah and his men where the enemy's lines were strongest. As a result, Uriah was killed in battle.

It had all started out as the perfect picture of romance and passion: a spring afternoon, a beautiful woman, and a handsome king. Now the picture had become splashed with broad, ugly strokes of deceit, treachery, betrayal, and even murder. It never fails. Sooner or later, *the main result of sin is more sin.*

Why is it that sin usually seems to breed more sin? Two reasons. First, like so many other areas of life, our resistance to sin is subject to the law of diminishing returns. This law is the principle at work when you watch a horror movie and don't get scared anymore.

The first time you saw a horror movie as a little kid, it scared the bejeebers out of you. You couldn't sleep for weeks. When you went back the next time, you knew what to expect and didn't get quite the same thrill. The next time you went, you laughed more than you screamed; and it didn't bother you at all. Now, your fear threshold is so high that if you don't walk away from the movie with bloodstains on your shirt, you don't feel like you've seen a horror flick.

The same thing happens with sin in our lives. The first time we're involved in something we know is against God's will, it really eats at our consciences. We feel bad. We feel convicted. But we rationalize our behavior, make excuses, and tell ourselves it was just this once. Of course, now that we've done it once, it's almost as if the boundary line has been moved back a bit. So we take one step further and then another and then another. And each time, the sin continues to erode our consciences little by little, until they almost don't exist.

The second factor that often causes sin to produce more sin is its ability to choke off our relationship with the only One who can help us really fight sin. Sin not only weakens our ability to recognize temptation, it also weakens our ability to resist it.

I was a high school student at a one-week camp in North Carolina. On the last day, everybody was herded onto the massive front porch of the conference center for a group picture. The group was so big that the picture had to be shot in two phases: first the right side of the group, then the left side.

Waiting for the photographer to set up his gear, I began to formulate a plan. I was standing in the upper right corner of the crowd when he shot the right side of the group. I decided to look left and wave my hand just as the camera clicked the picture.

Then, in the time it took the photographer to reset his camera for the left side of the group, I raced behind the bodies to take a place in the bottom left corner, looking across to the other side of the group with a wave and a smile. The next day, when we received the pictures as we mounted the buses for home, I was exhilarated that the plan had worked perfectly. The photograph showed me waving at myself from both ends of the picture.

That's how Satan uses sin in our lives. In studying David's life and temptation, we see that Satan doesn't stop with just one temptation. He works both ends of the picture.

First, he tempts us to sin. Then, after we've sinned, he's at the other end of the picture making us feel like jerks for sinning. We start to think, *There's no way God could forgive a sleazy sinner like me. I don't blame Him. I can't even forgive myself. People like Billy Graham deserve forgiveness, but then he probably never needs it. Me? I deserve to get nailed.*

Of course, with that kind of attitude, it's tough to maintain any kind of fellowship with God so that He can help us resist temptation. So that makes us even more vulnerable when Satan races back to the temptation end of the picture. Then, after we've dug ourselves deeper with more sin, Satan comes back from the other side of the porch to haunt us with how sinful we are and how we could not possibly be forgiven.

Breaking the Cycle

So how do we break the cycle? We do so by confessing our sin. We break it by remembering that God is a loving and gracious Father who never gives up on us and wants to restore fellowship with us. The Bible puts it this way: "If we claim to be without sin, we deceive ourselves and the truth is not in us. If we confess our sins, He is faithful and just and will forgive us our sins and purify us from all unrighteousness" (1 John 1:8-9).

Sin is always bad. It always breaks God's heart. But there is one thing worse than sin: unconfessed sin. And the main result of unconfessed sin is more sin. The only person who can stop that cycle is you. The question is: Will you do it?

15. The High Price of Sin

The want ad originally ran in a California newspaper: "For Sale: $200, Satan, pet South American boa constrictor. Educational, interesting, reasonably safe [and I love this line], loves children of all sizes!" The gentleman who placed the ad reported that he had gotten nine inquiries. Strangely enough, all of them were from women.

No one took much notice of the ad when it originally ran back in 1971. The advertisement ran, and the snake was sold. That was it—or so it appeared. It took an enterprising reporter to draw the connection between that want ad for Satan, the pet South American boa constrictor, and a headline in the morning newspaper of November 10, 1980: "Family's Pet Snake Squeezes 7 Month Infant to Death."

Apparently a man from the East bought the snake while he was out in California on business. He figured the snake would be a fun and unique gift for the kids when he got back home. At first, it was. It was unique and creative, fascinating and exciting. For a full nine years it seemed like a very wise purchase . . . until the early morning hours of that November night when Satan, the pet South American boa constrictor, squeezed the life out of the man's seven-month-old son.

Lesson Number Four: Sin Is Costly

Probably the most important lesson that David's life teaches us about sin is that it is costly. There will always be a price to pay. It may not be an immediate cost. It may be weeks or months or even years before we discover the results of our choices. What we can be sure of is that no matter how interesting or fun or fascinating or reasonably safe disobedience seems, eventually there will be a price to pay. Sooner or later, Satan puts the squeeze on us.

Solomon wrote, "The way of the unfaithful is hard" (Proverbs 13:15). Anyone who takes a careful look at David's life discovers how hard unfaithfulness can be when it is translated into human suffering and carried from one generation to the next.

About eight months went by before David confessed his sin of adultery with Bathsheba. From all appearances, we might assume that this was the final chapter in the Bathsheba scandal. But that would be naive.

When Nathan confronted David with a parable pointing to his sin, David responded with righteous indignation by saying that the rich man who had committed the offense should have to pay the penalty four times over. What he didn't realize was that he would have to face the consequences of his sin at least as many times. A quick look at the fallout from the affair with Bathsheba reminds us that there is no such thing as just a little sin.

David wanted very badly for the child he had conceived with Bathsheba to live. In one sense, he might have seen it as a way of paying back Uriah for his treacherous death. When the child died, David's emotional and mental turmoil exploded. It brought back all the guilt all over again, but the pain didn't stop there.

Not surprisingly, David's first born son, Ammon, exhibited some of the same bad habits and weaknesses that his father did. But he didn't look next door. Ammon raped his own sister, David's daughter Tamar.

Then, when David's second oldest son, Absalom, found out that his brother had raped his sister, he devised a way to kill his brother Ammon.

Not long after that, Absalom turned his rage toward his father, violently rebelling against David, even trying to kill him. But it was, in fact, Absalom who was killed when a freak accident in which his hair got caught in a tree left him an easy target for his enemies.

David's third-born son, Adonijah, hated his father so much that he tried to kill David when he was lying on his deathbed. But Adonijah was killed by David's youngest son Solomon.

From a small seedling of sin, planted in the passion and romance of a spring afternoon, blossomed pain, tragedy, misery, and death. Hadn't God forgiven David for his sin? Yes, but forgiveness is not a wave of the hand and a waiver of the laws of nature. God will forgive us if we confess our sins, but there are other parties who may not be so gracious. Nature does not always grant us second chances.

The Ugly Side of Sin

We don't often get this picture of sin do we? Usually the movies, the music, and the romance novels give us a picture of the passion. But they don't show us the product. They tell us a story, but they don't tell us the whole story.

I remember bugging my dad at the county fair to let me go into a tent that advertised all kinds of freak animals: the half chicken-half dog, five-legged cow, parakeet that barks, attack hamster exhibit. I felt it would be an enriching, educational experience. Besides, the sign out front said, "Free Admission."

Dad let me go in, and I made my way through the exhibit. But when I came to the exit at the other end of the tent, I saw the sign at the turnstyle: "Donations here, $2.00 minimum." I know now that I didn't have to pay, but I didn't know it then. It cost me the rest of my spending money to get away from that barking parakeet. Plus I was afraid they might send the hamster after me.

When I got out of the exhibit that night, crying, scared, and angry, Dad said something I'll never forget. "Son, don't forget that with most choices in life, you may not have to pay to enter. But you're going to have to pay before you leave."

The Forgotten Witness

Alfred Hitchcock was one of Hollywood's first and best directors of suspense movies. He had a knack for taking everyday events and surrounding them with a web of intrigue, drama, and mystery. One of the great Hitchcock techniques was to show us a murder scene in which someone was ruthlessly killed and lead us to believe, along with the murderer, that there were no witnesses. Then, as the camera pulls back, we realize that the whole drama was watched by an unsuspecting and unsuspected witness.

We get a hint of that same drama in 2 Samuel 11. We read how carefully and frantically David tried to cover his tracks with a lie here and a murder there. We get the impression that when Uriah died, David felt the nightmare ended. It was bloody and cruel, but it had to be done. Then it was over. He would marry Bathsheba, bring her into his house, and paint the whole sordid mess with a whitewash of honor.

Unfortunately, what David forgot—and what we too often forget—is that these events were played out in the sight of an all-knowing and holy God. "After the time of mourning was over, David had her brought to his house, and she became his wife and bore him a son. *But the thing David had done displeased the Lord*" (2 Samuel 11:27, italics mine).

Sin is never as simple and as easy as it first seems. It may look easy going in, but it won't look that way coming out. It's not a matter of trying to scare someone; it's a matter of trying to be realistic. Sin hurts the one who commits it, but the pain seldom stops there. Like a rock that's thrown into a peaceful lake, the ripples grow wider and wider. First sin affects our relationship with God. Then it affects our relationship with ourselves, then with family members and friends. The circles get wider and wider the more we splash and slap to cover the ripples.

It may have been that lingering memory of the Bathsheba episode and the high price paid that led David's son, Solomon, many years later to write, "There is a way that seems right to a man, but in the end it leads to death" (Proverbs 14:12).

Is that the direction in which you're moving? If so, you don't need to reach that destination. There's help before you get there.

Something to Think About

1. Suppose David wanted to retrace his steps and figure out where he had gotten off the path. Where in the process of sin do you think he went wrong?

2. What are some of the situations in your life that take you close to the edge of temptation?

3. What are some ways that you can protect yourself from temptation?

4. This section dealt with some of the consequences of sin and the high price of disobedience. What are some of the costs that you personally have had to pay for the sin in your life?

SECTION FIVE:

AFTER GOD'S OWN HEART

Have mercy on me, O God, according to Your unfailing love; according to Your great compassion blot out my transgressions. Wash away all my iniquity and cleanse me from my sin. For I know my transgressions, and my sin is always before me. Against You, You only, have I sinned and done what is evil in Your sight, so that You are proved right when You speak and justified when You judge.

Create in me a pure heart, O God, and renew a steadfast spirit within me. Do not cast me from Your presence or take Your Holy Spirit from me. Restore to me the joy of Your salvation and grant me a willing spirit, to sustain me.

(Psalm 51:1-4, 10-12)

16. True Confessions

Most people who study the life of David become convinced by this point that the guy was first-class slime. They want to put his picture in the dictionary next to the word *sleazeball* (slēz′-bòl, n.). It doesn't take a genius to observe that Saul may have made some big mistakes, but he never committed adultery and murder. Granted, he may have been a wasted paper clip, but at least he wasn't out wasting people!

It almost seems unfair. Saul botched up a sacrifice before he went into battle, and Samuel freaked out. Then David sacrificed the life of one of his top officers, Uriah; and Nathan decided to tell him a story about sheep. It doesn't make sense. If we were making an honest comparison between the two men, frankly, most of us would peg Saul as the one after

God's own heart and David as the wasted paper clip. Did Saul get a bum rap?

David's Confession

Before you read any further, take a moment to look at Psalm 51. It's here that we really see the difference between Saul and David, the difference between a hardhearted King Saul and a brokenhearted King David. Listen to the words of a man whose heart has been broken before God. This guy's not using any religious sin screen; he's just falling before God and crying out for forgiveness. It's in David's prayer that we quite literally get the inside story.

> Have mercy on me, O God, according to Your unfailing love; according to Your great compassion blot out my transgressions. Wash away all my iniquity and cleanse me from my sin. For I know my transgressions, my sin is always before me. Against You, You only, have I sinned and done what is evil in Your sight, so that You are proved right when You speak and justified when You judge. . . .
>
> Create in me a pure heart, O God, and renew a steadfast spirit within me. Do not cast me from Your presence or take Your Holy Spirit from me. Restore to me the joy of Your salvation and grant me a willing spirit, to sustain me. . . .
>
> You do not delight in sacrifice, or I would bring it; You do not take pleasure in burnt offerings. The sacrifices of God are a broken spirit; a broken and contrite heart, O God, You will not despise (Psalm 51:1-4, 10-12, 16-17).

When we shuck it right down, the only real difference between Saul and David is that one man sought to cover his sin and the other man sought to confess it. Both men made some serious mistakes. Both men displeased God. But only one finally came back and offered to God a prayer of true confession.

Confession doesn't come easy to any of us. It's never fun to admit we're going the wrong way and then accept responsibility for turning things around. Most of us are like the Presbyterian preacher that Peter Cartwright wrote about in his autobiography. Cartwright, an old Methodist circuit rider who traveled and ministered over thousands of miles of untamed backcountry in the early 1800s, was a real character.

He wrote about one occasion when he showed up at a church meeting in time to hear this Presbyterian preacher deliver a powerful sermon. But when he got to the end of his message, he began to apologize to the congregation for a recent episode of public drunkenness during which he made a fool of himself in front of the whole town.

It was bad enough that the guy got sloppy drunk, but what blew Cartwright away was the man's watered-down confession. This brother explained to the congregation that his mother had wrestled with the same problem of strong drink and that she had been more than a little dependent on the bottle during those long days of pregnancy. He went on to say that she had assured him that his failing was an inherited trait and that he would probably never be able to overcome it.

That was when Cartwright stood up in front of the whole congregation and made his own statement.

Cartwright reported that he rose to tell all present:

> I thought the preacher's apology for drunkenness was infinitely worse than the act itself; that I looked upon it as a lie, and a downright slander of his mother; and that I believed his love of whiskey was the result of unwise use of it . . . that I feared the preacher would live and die a drunkard, and be damned at last, and that I hoped the people there would not continue to receive him as their preacher until he gave them ample evidence that he was entirely cured of drunkenness!

Cartwright was a shy, little guy; but you always knew what was on his mind.

David in Quicksand

It had been about eight months since David had his fling with Bathsheba. Uriah was dead, the baby had died, and now David had begun to die on the inside. Torn up by the loss of his child and the guilt of sin, it had been a very unpleasant eight months. David described those months this way: "When I kept silent, my bones wasted away through my groaning all day long. For day and night Your hand was heavy upon me; my strength was sapped as in the heat of summer" (Psalm 32:3-4).

Sometimes we can fool other people about our own guilt and innocence, but David's story reminds us that we can only fool ourselves for so long. We might be able to rationalize for a while and maybe eventually put the guilt out of our minds and make it disappear altogether. But guilt has a way of making itself known, sometimes through something as minor as beads of sweat on your forehead (like when you were the one who put the rabbit pellets in your sister's Cocoa Puffs) or an accelerated heartbeat (like when your mother asked if this was your idea of a joke to tease your sister that way).

But other times guilt raises its head through what on the surface might look like totally unrelated symptoms. For example, sometimes we expose our guilt by being overly sensitive to criticism. Other times we betray our sense of guilt by being overly legalistic and harsh toward others' misdeeds. (Note David's response to Nathan's story of the rich man who gave away the poor man's lamb: "He must pay for that lamb four times over" [2 Samuel 12:6].) Probably one of the most common causes of ulcers and chronic fatigue is guilt that has been confessed.

One of the major effects of sin that I've seen have been responses to guilt over sexual sin. Just recently, I spoke with a beautiful, newlywed girl who was not able to enjoy sex with her husband because she was haunted by painful memories from previous relationships.

Sin is like quicksand. At first it only affects one part of you, but before long it starts to swallow you up. For eight months David had been sinking deeper and deeper. It looked like he might be another paper clip down for the count.

God Makes the First Move

With David staggering under the load of his sin, the Bible says, "The Lord sent Nathan to David" (2 Samuel 12:1). I have to stop to point out that this action is what blows me away about God's love. David was the perfect sleazeball, ignoring God, trying to deny his guilt, and running from the situation as fast as he could. So who made the first move to bring him back to wholeness? "The Lord sent Nathan to David." David didn't summon Nathan and say, "OK, let's get this thing out in the open; I can't take it anymore." The Lord made the first move. That just amazes me. If I had been the Lord, I would have sent somebody to David all right, but it would have been the ghost of Uriah or The Equalizer or somebody like that.

One of the great truths that unfolds from David's tragedy like a colorful banner against a dark sky is the fact that there is no sin that God is not willing to forgive. There is no quicksand so deep that God's forgiveness is not deeper still. The only sin that God can't forgive is the sin that goes unconfessed.

It just might be that someone reading these words needs to hear this truth. We sometimes think that we are so sinful, so lost, so bad that God has lost interest and given up on us. But nothing could be further from the truth. Maybe you're reading these words right now because the Lord sent Duffy to you. (Doesn't sound quite the same, does it?)

When we're sinking in quicksand, it doesn't do any good to grab more sand. We might be able to claw and fight to stay afloat a few more minutes, but eventually we're going down. Neither does it do any good to start throwing mud at others and blaming them for the mess. The only way to get out of quicksand is to reach for something solid from above.

Looking back on this messy episode some time later, David explained it in these words: "I waited patiently for the Lord; He turned to me and heard my cry. He lifted me out of the slimy pit, out of the mud and mire; He set my feet on a rock and gave me a firm place to stand" (Psalm 40:1-2).

God can do the same for you.

17. To Tell the Truth

Whenever anyone files an insurance claim for a traffic accident, he has to fill out detailed reports explaining exactly what happened and why. These reports are then sent to the Pain-in-the-Neck Division of the local insurance company which then reports back about why the filer won't be getting any help. It's really a neat system!

Sometimes the insurance investigators who read these reports get some classic stories. Some time ago, the *Toronto Sun* printed a few of the actual samples from an insurance company's files:

> "In my attempt to kill a fly, I drove into a telephone pole."
>
> "I had been driving my car for forty years

when I fell asleep at the steering wheel and had an accident."

"The pedestrian had no idea which direction to go; so I ran over him."

"The telephone pole was approaching fast. I was attempting to swerve out of its path when it struck my front end."

"Coming home, I drove into the wrong house and collided with a tree I don't have."

"The guy was all over the road. I had to swerve a number of times before I hit him."

"An invisible car came out of nowhere, struck my vehicle and vanished."

"The indirect cause of this accident was a little guy in a small car with a big mouth."

A Prayer of Confession

Most of us seem to have a tough time confessing guilt, admitting fault, and accepting blame. David's prayer of confession in Psalm 51 helps us to see what it really means to genuinely confess our sin to God. We've looked at it already, but it deserves a repeated reading.

> Have mercy on me, O God, according to Your unfailing love; according to Your great compassion blot out my transgressions. Wash away all my iniquity and cleanse me from my sin. For I know my transgressions and my sin is always before me. Against You, You only, have I sinned and done what is evil in Your sight, so that You are proved right when You speak and justified when You judge. . . .
>
> Create in me a pure heart, O God, and renew

a steadfast spirit within me. Do not cast me from Your presence or take Your Holy Spirit from me. Restore to me the joy of Your salvation and grant me a willing spirit, to sustain me" (Psalm 51:1-4, 10-12).

The first thing that immediately strikes us about David's prayer of confession is that he obviously recognizes he has sinned and that his sin is a direct offense to a holy God. We're not really prepared for confession unless we begin there.

We live in a culture that misunderstands the fact that sin is a grave and serious offense against God. That's partially because we don't really understand who God is. We think of God as some kind of George Burns figure who sits up in heaven and snickers at our sin: "Doggone, look at those humans, would you? Ain't they somethin'?" We don't worship a Father in heaven. As C.S. Lewis put it, We worship a "Grandfather in heaven," a senile old guy who's nice enough but essentially harmless.

David's prayer reflects an understanding that every sin we commit, every act or thought of disobedience, is not just some kind of station-to-station violation. It is a person-to-Person offense. It's not just a matter of breaking God's laws; it's a matter of breaking God's heart. David prayed, "Against You, You only, have I sinned and done what is evil in Your sight, so that You're proved right when You speak and justified when You judge" (Psalm 51:4).

Now, I don't know about you, but when I read that prayer, I think, *How can he say, "Against You,* You only, *have I sinned"?* I'm not too sure that Uriah would go along with that assessment. And what about

Bathsheba, Joab, and who knows how many others? But the bottom line with any sin is that it is first and foremost an offense against God. He made the laws that David broke, and He made the people that David hurt. The primary offense was against Him.

The best way to understand this truth is to think back to all the times you made your little brother (or sister) eat a marble or stick a marshmallow in his ear or when you "accidentally" knocked his toothbrush in the toilet. You will probably remember that even though the offense affected only your little brother, your parents took it personally.

I can distinctly recall when I locked my brother out of the house one day. My parents responded as if they had been the ones stuck out in the summer sun for four hours. Needless to say, I hadn't done any such thing to them. No marbles, no marshmallows, not even so much as a chocolate chip in their ears. But to commit an offense against my brother was to commit an offense against my father. He made the rules; he was in authority. We were his children, and he was the one who administered justice. Consequently, while my brother was licking the marshmallow off his cheeks, my dad was giving me a licking on my "cheeks."

To really have a proper attitude for confession, we need to understand this: All sin is sin against God. It was that attitude that encouraged David to exhibit the three essentials of true confession.

Calling a Spade a Spade

Have you ever had someone apologize to you but not really apologize? Or have you ever had someone ask your forgiveness; but when he was through, you felt like *you* had done something wrong? For example: "I'm really sorry I copied those answers off your test and got you in trouble. I guess I couldn't believe you weren't careful enough to cover them up so others couldn't see." Or "I'm sorry I ran over your bicycle. It seems like people would pass a law to keep something so hard to see off the streets."

That's the kind of confession that most of us know all too well. It's the I'm-sorry-but-it's-your-fault or the I'm-sorry-but-that's-just-the-way-I-am motif—the kind of nonconfession confession that means nothing.

From the very first words of David's prayer in Psalm 51, it's obvious that David accepted full responsibility for his sin. He didn't try to shift the blame to someone else. One of the truest marks of genuine confession is not trying to tiptoe away from the blame. Notice how many times David used the first person pronoun: "Have mercy on *me,* O God . . . blot out *my* transgressions [sins]. Wash away all *my* iniquity and cleanse *me* from *my* sin. For I know *my* transgressions, and *my* sin is always before me" (italics added).

Remember Saul after that big snafu when the Philistines had surrounded Israel? Saul told Samuel:

> "When I saw that the men were scattering, and that you did not come at the set time, and that the Philistines were assembling at Micmash, I thought, 'Now the Philistines will come down against me at Gilgal, and I have not sought the Lord's favor.' So I felt compelled to offer the burnt offering" (1 Samuel 13:12).

Saul couldn't bring himself to admit that he just blew

it, that he caved in to pressure from the crowd and disobeyed God. Instead it was everybody else's fault. That's not true confession. That's fancy footwork.

If anyone had reason to shift blame, David did. After all, Bathsheba didn't have to go to the King's palace. She wasn't exactly innocent. As they say, "it takes two to tango," and she was a big girl. We can imagine the conversation:

David's Messenger:	" 'Scuse me, Ma'am, but the King is over there on the roof of the palace watching you bathe. He'd like to know if you would come over."
Bathsheba:	"To the King's palace? Oh, I haven't a thing to wear."
David's Messenger:	"I think that's what the King had in mind, Ma'am."
Bathsheba:	"Well, OK. I wonder what he wants to talk about."

David never attempted to blame anyone else for his sin. He didn't blame Bathsheba for being promiscuous. He didn't blame his father for making him spend all of his formative years around sheep. He didn't blame Nathan the prophet for making him feel false guilt. He blamed himself. He called a spade a spade. That's true confession.

Willing to Hear Bad News

A second mark of true confession is the way we respond to correction. When Nathan went to the palace to confront David about his adultery with Bathsheba, he knew it could go either way. One didn't just go into the throne room and tell the King he'd better clean up his act. That would be like going to Darth Vader and telling him he dresses funny. There was no way to know how David might respond.

David's response was one of humility and repentance: "I have sinned against the Lord" (2 Samuel 12:13). He didn't start accusing Nathan of being judgmental or holier-than-thou, although it might have been funny if he had:

Nathan: "What you did with Bathsheba, David, was adultery; and you know it."
David: "Oh yeah? Well, who made you the Prophet of Israel?
Nathan: "God did."
David: "He did (his voice cracking)? Uh . . . OK."

David accepted Nathan's correction as a message from God. He wasn't happy about it; he wasn't glad to hear it. He didn't say, "Oh please, tell me more!" But he was willing to listen.

Every now and then Scripture talks about someone being hardhearted. This description is not a reference to high cholesterol or hardening of the arteries. It is a reference to the fact that some people simply cannot hear correction.

When God speaks to us through our consciences, Bible studies, or friends, think of it as sunlight shining into the darkness of disobedience. What happens in response to that word of correction depends on the makeup of our hearts. For example, when sunlight hits snow, it softens it. When sunlight hits clay, it hardens it. It's the same sunlight in both cases; the difference is in the object.

True confession comes from the kind of heart that can be melted by God's correction. In Psalm 51, David prayed: "The sacrifices of God are a broken spirit; a broken and contrite [humble] heart, O God, You will not despise" (v. 17).

When a parent or a youth pastor corrects you, how do you respond? When a friend tries to speak to you about something he or she is seeing in your life, do you answer back by saying, "Well, at least I don't ________________ like you do"? If your pastor preaches a message that deals with your sin, are you able to humbly accept the word of correction? Or do you complain about how he's always trying to make us feel guilty?

There will be times, however, when we are falsely accused; and we can take the criticism lightly. But we should also recognize that the person correcting us may be a "Nathan" sent from God. How we respond to that word of correction can make all the difference between confession that's real and confession that's real weak.

Repent or Resent

Before I became a Christian, I remember seeing church buses that looked like they had been used for troop movement during World War I. They were junky-looking, run-down, and losing paint. On the side of the bus was the name of the church in big bold letters. Somewhere on the back, someone had carefully, solemnly painted the word *Repent.* I used to joke to my friends that the word should be *Repaint.*

When most of us hear the word *repent* we think of sawdust trails, 30 verses of "Just as I Am," and a Bible-thumping preacher who sweats a lot. Repentance has gotten a lot of bad press in our culture because we often associate it with manipulation, fear tactics, and too-slick evangelists. But repentance is an absolute essential for true confession.

Basically, to repent means to change your mind. It comes from two words which mean to rethink or think again. When we repent, what we really say is this: "God, I didn't use to think this type of attitude or action was all that bad. I didn't really think it was sinful, and I didn't really care whether or not You did. But now I am beginning to understand that You judge this attitude or action as sinful and that You are right in making that judgment. In fact, I've had a change of heart; and I agree with You." But it's a lot easier just to say, "I repent!"

Actually, saying "I repent" really isn't that easy, is it? When most of us begin to realize that we've disobeyed God, our first instinct is to resent God's law. We're not really sorry we've sinned; we're just sorry we got caught. We want to excuse ourselves, blame it on someone else, or gloss over the whole thing as a little slip. But true confession happens when we move from resenting to repenting.

When David prayed his prayer of confession in Psalm 51, he showed every sign of repentance:

> "I know my transgressions, and my sin is always before me. Against You, You only, have I sinned and done what is evil in Your sight, so that You are proved right when You speak and justified when You judge" (vv. 3-4).

Get it? David didn't say, "Come on, Lord, lighten up. So what's a little adultery and murder? Where's

Your sense of humor? I mean, this was just a little slip. When I did all that stuff, it wasn't the real me. The real me is a guy after Your own heart, remember? You know, David? Beloved? The guy who kills giants?"

David just shucks it right down: "I was sinful at birth, sinful from the time my mother conceived me" (Psalm 51:5). In other words, "This wasn't a slipup; it was the real me. And I need You, Lord, to change the real me." "Create in me a pure heart, O God, and renew a steadfast spirit within me" (Psalm 51:10).

Cover or Confess

A hundred times a week, life offers us opportunities to cover or confess. Sometimes it's just stupid stuff. You may be hanging out with your friends; everybody's talking and laughing. Then all of a sudden, there is an extremely offensive smell. Almost immediately, someone shouts, "OK, who did it?"

Or you just spilled salad dressing on the tablecloth at a fancy restaurant: Do you call the waiter over and admit that you tossed your own salad, or do you act coy and slide your plate over the stain?

Sometimes it really doesn't matter whether we decide to cover or confess. When it comes to sin, though, that confession can make the difference between a person God can use and just another wasted paper clip.

It's possible that there are some areas of your life that have been seriously stained by sin. My prayer is that you won't try to cover them up with dumb excuses, phony religion, or blaming other people. There's incredible freedom in true confession. Why don't you slowly reread Psalm 51 right now and make it your own prayer of confession?

Something to Think About

1. Why do we have such a hard time with confession? Why would someone like David tolerate eight months of intense pain before he confessed and repented of his sin?

2. What are some of the ways guilt affects our relationships with other people? What do these effects teach us about the way sin affects our relationship with God?

3. Which of the elements of true confession is toughest for you? Why?

4. What are some of the ways you attempt to cover up your wrong doings?

5. If Jesus walked up behind you as you were reading this chapter, which part do you think He might ask you to read over again? Why?

18. It's How You Play the Game

Have you ever watched a movie so powerful that even after it ended and the room cleared you were still there, glued to your seat? That happened to me recently, and it was embarrassing when my children couldn't get me to wake up!

I think there is that same sense of awe and wonder when we read through David's story. Lots of characters walk across the stage in First and Second Samuel: Samuel, Saul, Mephibosheth, Bathsheba, Nathan, and Uriah to name only a few. Having listened to and watched this real life drama, it's hard at first to get up and move on. It leaves us with questions and ideas, and it may even trouble us a bit.

That's OK. Sometimes a good story will do that. We begin to identify with the characters and experience the drama with them—both the victories and the defeats. But as we leave these chapters in the life of David, my prayer is that we'll walk out of this book with a renewed sense of challenge and encouragement.

First: A Word of Challenge

I'm a big fan of college basketball. In fact, I'm such a fanatic that I go through my calendar in December and write in all of the games through March that I'm going to watch on TV. I know, that's pretty bad. But we have to set some priorities, don't we?

So many times I watch a team that has great outside shooting, good ball-handling, and a strong defense. But they experience defeat because, in the language of the sport, they have a weak inside game. That description means a team is not able to control the play right under the basket. They don't get the rebounds; they don't set the screens; they don't block out.

If there is one major lesson to learn from the lives of Saul and David, it is the importance of the inside game; cultivating a heart that is sensitive and obedient to God, screening out temptation, blocking out sin, and learning how to rebound from disobedience.

We may be great at witnessing, praying, or Scripture memory. We may be active in the youth choir or on the leadership team. These activities are important. But if there is a weakness on the inside—in the heart—we can be sure that the Enemy will try to exploit that weakness to cause defeat.

For me, it's like rock climbing. I enjoy taking my students out to a high rock face for a day of climbing. It's fun; it's exciting; and it teaches them to pray! But I always give them one word of caution while we're out there on the rocks: Be careful not to step on the ropes.

Climbing ropes are a vital, lifesaving piece of equipment as long as they are in good shape. In fact, the tensile strength of a good climbing rope is about 8,000 pounds. That means it's designed not to snap and break if it's holding any weight under 8,000 pounds. That might not sound like much, but the human body has a tensile strength of about 3,000 pounds. So your body will snap before the rope does. Encouraging, isn't it?

However, there is one thing that is deadly to climbing ropes: the grinding action of little pieces of rock and sand. When someone steps on a climbing rope, that action grinds into that rope little, unseen pieces of rock and sand that start to rot it from the inside. You won't see the breakdown, of course. You won't even notice it until someday there is extra tension in that rope when someone slips or falls. It's at that point that the rope will snap. It's a fall that begins because of a breakdown on the inside.

There is a lesson to be learned here. David's life reminds us that we need to concentrate consistently on the inside game—praying, spending time with God, and reading the Word. Most falls begin with rot on the inside where no one notices. The grinding and breakdown continues until finally there is some slip or tension, and that's when the fall comes. Solomon put it this way: "Above all else, guard your heart, for it is the wellspring of life" (Proverbs 4:23).

Second: A Word of Encouragement

If we were out on the playground of an elementary school choosing sides for a game of old-fashioned

Bible Hero, common sense tells us that David wouldn't go very early in the choosing. Who wants to have a guy on his team who has committed adultery and murder and has broken just about every other commandment in the Book? It's obvious he has a problem. We can imagine David standing next to the backstop while someone says, "OK, we'll take David. But you have to give us Elijah and the Apostle Paul."

Yet David is described as a man after God's own heart (1 Samuel 13:14). How can that be? Why did God choose a loser like David to make him King of Israel? Because the key to walking with God is not always being the winner. They key to walking with God is realizing what He can do with "losers."

As we look back at David's life, we can see from the big picture that David's story is not about some stained-glass saints who never made mistakes. David's mistakes and sins are documented in vivid, full-color honesty by the writers of Scripture. There are both successes and failures from the Scripture's account of David's long life that we haven't even explored. But what we have seen has presented plenty of evidence that David was a normal person with normal hopes, hassles, hang-ups, and hormones).

Maybe that's why he has become my hero. When I look at David, I realize how much God can do with people just like me if we hang on to Him and hang in for the long haul.

Direction Is More Important than Position

I spend a lot of time talking to teenagers about God. Sometimes I speak at a conference. Sometimes it's a ski weekend. Sometimes it's a summer camp. Over and over, I get excited when I see teens respond to biblical truth.

I remember one occasion on the last night of a seven-day backpacking trip with my youth group. It had been a great six days of backpacking, rock climbing, white-water rafting, and living together. We had a special tradition on the last night of our trips; we always share in a special foot-washing service around the campfire.

Now, that might sound weird, but it was really simple. One at a time, each student came over and washed my feet. OK, I'm only kidding. What they actually did was wash one another's feet. Needless to say, to walk over and wash someone's feet after he or she spent six days hiking the Appalachian Trail is no picnic! It was probably more than emotion that made our eyes water as we shared together around that campfire.

I can still remember watching Cheryl as she stepped around the fire and moved in Dana's direction. It had been a hard week for Dana. She had complained about everything: The trail was too steep (I explained that that's why they're called mountains), the food was lousy ("That's because this is a youth-group function"), and her pack was too heavy (I finally agreed to carry my own tent). You name it, she griped about it. I guess that's what all of us were thinking when Cheryl knelt down to wash Dana's feet.

Dana must have been thinking about it too. Because when Cheryl began to wash her feet, I could see the tears start to form in her eyes. Then the tears rolling down her cheeks began to glow in the light of our campfire. By the time Cheryl had embraced Dana and began to move back to her place in the circle, Dana was openly weeping.

At first no one said anything. No one had to. Then Dana blurted out between sobs, "I've got to say something. All this week I know I've been acting like a . . . a . . . a . . . big witch. And I know you guys have been trying to love me and reach out to me anyway. I want you all to know that just now when Cheryl hugged me—I know this sounds weird—but I felt Jesus put His arms around me and hug me. It's like Jesus is saying, 'I love you, Dana, no matter what.' Thanks to all of you, I'll never forget this week or this night."

I think we were all shocked at first. Maybe some of us were even a little ticked that Jesus would hug somebody like Dana. After all, there were a lot of us around the circle who hadn't been jerks all week. How come *we* weren't getting hugged by Jesus?

Mostly I was excited. I had been praying for Dana for a long time. I guess I'm a pretty typical youth worker. When I hear a student testify like that, I'm calm on the outside. But on the inside I'm thinking *Yeah, God! Sic'em, Lord!* Yet even as I sat there smiling, there was a part of me that was more cautious.

I knew that as special as this night was, it wasn't the whole story. Somehow we were going to have to help Dana translate the experience of this night into her daily life back home, and that wouldn't be easy. I had been on her campus a lot, and I knew that kids weren't likely to stop her in the hall and say, "I know this sounds strange, but I'd like to wash your feet." I knew that what had happened around our fire was important, but I also knew that it was only one step in a very long walk.

One of the lessons we learn as we look at the big picture of David's life is that God deals with us over the long haul. He rejoices over every step forward, and He agonizes over every step backward. But He also knows that our current position is not nearly as important as our long-term direction.

Saul began his life with a heart that was warm toward God. When God first called Saul through the Prophet Samuel, it was as if he had genuinely felt God put His arms around him (1 Samuel 9–10). But the committed life is not lived in the past. What is important is where Saul went as he moved away from that day of anointing.

David's life had ups and downs with some very dark chapters of sin and disobedience. So did Saul's. So did a lot of other people's. Why didn't God give up on David? Because through all of the bad times and the good times, David never stopped walking with God. To be sure, he stalled a while; but the basic direction of his life was long-term commitment to God.

There were times when he went in the wrong direction, and that was bad. He had to pay a very high price for the times he strayed. However, the key question posed to us by David's life is not "Where are you in your walk with Christ now?" Rather, it is, "Where are you going to be five years or ten years from now in your walk with Christ?" ***It's not so much a matter of position as it is of direction.***

If you think back through Scripture, every one of the great saints of the Bible had some dark chapters. There are stories of drunkenness, lying, cowardice, disobedience, and failure. But one chapter doesn't make the whole story. If we confess and repent of our disobedience, God is more than willing to forgive us for our sin and help us up so we can move on in the journey.

Does that mean that what we do with Christ now is unimportant? No way! Our response to Christ now is critical. Because of the effects of sin and the law of diminishing returns in our disobedience, we shouldn't dare take this commitment lightly.

That was probably the mistake Saul made, assuming that sooner or later, he could get everything under control and then he would start obeying God. But it doesn't work that way. If we ignore what God is doing in our lives right now, we may discover that today's milestone will become tomorrow's tombstone.

But, the Bible teaches that there is hope for all of us in God's love and grace. It's not so much a question of whether we're winners or losers; it's a question of how we play the game. We tend to look at our lives and get discouraged. *How could God choose someone like me to do anything for Him?* We think, *I'm not very spiritual sometimes. I don't know the Bible very well, and I've had more than my share of disobedience and sin. I would have been the one on the palace rooftop saying to David, "Hey, let somebody else have a look!"*

The great lesson from David's life is that God never gives up on us. He knows that one step forward is not the whole journey, but he also knows that three steps backward are not the end of the journey either. God does not get discouraged by where we are now in our commitment. He is thinking long term: *Where are they headed?*

Remember that the story of David is *your* story. You are also beloved of God. Watch and listen so this very same God can make you into the grand design for which you were created. The promise is too great and the potential is too real to settle for being just one more wasted paper clip!